Vegetables & Salads

Vegetables & Salads

This edition first published in 1989
exclusively for Marks and Spencer p.l.c.
by arrangement with
the Octopus Publishing Group
Michelin House, 81 Fulham Road
London SW3 6RB
© Hennerwood Publications Limited, 1989
ISBN 0 86273 539 4
Printed in Spain by Imprenta Hispano-Americana, Barcelona

Contents

Soups

◆

A light vegetable soup makes a perfect first course, and there are some delicious recipes to choose from in this chapter. Smooth puréed soups such as Minted Lettuce Soup, Carrot & Coriander Soup or Cream of Cauliflower Soup can be served as an elegant beginning for a special dinner. Chilled creamy soups made with mushrooms and walnuts, or tomatoes and herbs are ideal starters for warmer days.

Hearty soups, smooth in texture or full of chunky vegetables, are almost meals in themselves, needing only some bread and cheese to accompany them. Main dish soups here include a chowder of sweetcorn, bacon and potatoes, a smooth thick soup based on nutritious root vegetables, a filling lentil and ham soup topped with crunchy croûtons, and a colourful mixture of garden vegetables with bacon and macaroni.

Tomato Vichysoisse (see recipe on page 8).

TOMATO VICHYSSOISE

This soup makes a delicious starter for a
barbecue meal or for a picnic.

40g (1½oz) butter
1 medium onion, peeled and finely chopped
350g (12oz) potatoes, peeled and roughly
  chopped
350g (12oz) tomatoes, roughly chopped
1 garlic clove, peeled and crushed
1 tablespoon tomato purée
1 tablespoon chopped fresh basil (optional)
450ml (¾ pint) chicken stock
450ml (¾ pint) milk
salt
freshly ground black pepper
150ml (¼ pint) double cream
chopped fresh parsley or basil, to garnish

Preparation time: 15 minutes, plus chilling
Cooking time: 30–35 minutes

1. Heat the butter in a pan, add the onion and
fry gently for 3 minutes. Add the potatoes,
tomatoes, garlic, tomato purée, basil, stock,
milk, and salt and pepper to taste. Bring to the
boil and simmer for 25–30 minutes.
2. Purée the soup in a blender or food
processor, or work through a sieve. Allow to
cool, then stir in the cream.
3. Chill the soup thoroughly. Garnish with the
chopped parsley or basil.

Serves 6

Nutrition content per serving   Carbohydrate: 17g   Fat: 20g
Fibre: 2g   Kilocalories: 267

CHINESE LEAF & PEPPER SOUP

2 tablespoons vegetable oil
50g (2oz) butter
225g (8oz) green peppers, cored, seeded and diced
2 onions, peeled and chopped
½ head Chinese leaves, shredded
40g (1½oz) plain flour
450ml (¾ pint) chicken stock
salt
freshly ground black pepper
450ml (¾ pint) milk
3 tablespoons single cream

Preparation time: 25 minutes
Cooking time: 45 minutes

1. Heat the oil in a saucepan, then add the
butter. Add the peppers, onion and Chinese
leaves and cook gently for 5 minutes.
2. Blend in the flour and cook for 1 minute.
Stir in the stock and bring to the boil. Add salt
and pepper and simmer, covered, for 30
minutes or until the vegetables are tender.
3. Purée the soup in a blender or food
processor, or work through a sieve. Return to
the pan, stir in the milk and heat through.
Taste and adjust seasoning and just before
serving, swirl in the cream.

Serves 4

Nutrition content per serving   Carbohydrate: 21g   Fat: 25g
Fibre: 5g   Kilocalories: 339

GARDENER'S BROTH

1 lean bacon rasher, rind removed, diced
25g (1oz) butter
2–3 small onions, peeled and sliced
2–3 small carrots, peeled and sliced
a small piece of turnip, chopped
1 litre (1¾ pints) stock or water
2 tomatoes, skinned and sliced
2–3 runner beans, topped and tailed
a few leaves young cabbage, shredded
salt
freshly ground black pepper
pinch of mixed herbs
25g (1oz) short-cut macaroni
grated cheese, to sprinkle
1 tablespoon finely chopped fresh parsley

Preparation time: 30 minutes
Cooking time: 1¼ hours

1. Put the bacon in a pan with the butter and
onions and sauté until soft. Add the carrot and
turnip and cook for a further 5 minutes. Pour
in the stock or water and bring to the boil.
2. Add the rest of the vegetables, salt and
pepper to taste, and herbs, then cover and
simmer for 45 minutes. Add the macaroni and
simmer for a further 15 minutes.
3. Serve piping hot sprinkled with grated
cheese and chopped parsley.

Serves 4

Nutrition content per serving   Carbohydrate: 12g   Fat: 9g
Fibre: 4g   Kilocalories: 153

TOP: Gardener's Broth; BOTTOM: Chinese Leaf &
Pepper Soup.

BORSHCH

25g (1oz) butter
1 large onion, peeled and sliced
1 large carrot, peeled and shredded
2 large cooked beetroots, sliced
½ small red cabbage, shredded
1.2 litres (2 pints) beef stock, skimmed of fat
1 tablespoon tomato purée
1 tablespoon malt vinegar
1 tablespoon sugar
salt
freshly ground black pepper
parsley sprig, to garnish
300ml (½ pint) soured cream, to finish

Preparation time: 20 minutes
Cooking time: 30–40 minutes

1. Melt the butter in a large saucepan. Add the vegetables, cover and cook gently for 5 minutes.
2. Stir in the remaining ingredients and bring to the boil. Cover and simmer for 20–30 minutes or until the vegetables are tender.
3. Adjust the seasoning and serve garnished with parsley and with the soured cream.

Serves 4

Nutrition content per serving   Carbohydrate: 17g   Fat: 21g
Fibre: 5g   Kilocalories: 272

MUSHROOM & WALNUT SOUP

25g (1oz) walnut pieces
25g (1oz) butter
1 medium onion, peeled and chopped
100g (4oz) button mushrooms, roughly chopped
900ml (1½ pints) chicken stock
large pinch of grated nutmeg
salt
freshly ground black pepper
6 tablespoons double cream
TO GARNISH:
chopped fresh chives
chopped walnuts

Preparation time: 10 minutes
Cooking time: 25 minutes

1. Cover the walnuts with boiling water and leave for 1 minute. Drain on paper towels.
2. Melt the butter in a medium saucepan, add the onion and fry until soft. Add the mushrooms and cook for 1 minute. Stir in the

stock, nutmeg, salt and pepper and bring to the boil. Cover and simmer for 15 minutes.
3. Chop the walnuts in a blender or food processor. Add the cooked vegetables and liquid and blend until the mushrooms are finely chopped. Adjust the seasoning. Chill well.
4. To serve, stir the cream into the soup and sprinkle with the chives and walnuts.

Serves 4

Nutrition content per serving   Carbohydrate: 2g   Fat: 19g
Fibre: 1g   Kilocalories: 188

SWEETCORN & BACON SOUP

25g (1oz) butter
75g (3oz) streaky bacon, rind removed, diced
1 onion, peeled and chopped
1 garlic clove, peeled and chopped
1 carrot, peeled and chopped
1 celery stick, chopped
1.75 litres (3 pints) chicken stock
450g (1lb) potatoes, peeled and cubed
1 × 350g (12oz) can sweetcorn kernels, drained
salt
freshly ground black pepper
2 tablespoons chopped fresh parsley
½ green pepper, cored, seeded and thinly sliced

Preparation time: 15 minutes
Cooking time: 45 minutes

1. Melt the butter in a large saucepan, add the bacon and fry until crisp. Remove the bacon with a slotted spoon and set on one side.
2. Add the onion and garlic to the pan and fry gently in the butter and bacon fat until softened. Add the carrot and celery and fry for a further minute.
3. Add the stock, potatoes and two-thirds of the sweetcorn with salt and pepper. Bring to the boil, skimming if necessary, and simmer for 15 minutes or until the potatoes are soft.
4. Allow to cool for a few minutes, then purée in a blender or food processor, or work through a sieve. Return to the rinsed pan and stir in the parsley, green pepper, reserved bacon and remaining sweetcorn. Reheat gently.

Serves 6

Nutrition content per serving   Carbohydrate: 24g   Fat: 8g
Fibre: 5g   Kilocalories: 177

TOP: Borsch; MIDDLE: Mushroom & Walnut Soup;
BOTTOM: Sweetcorn & Bacon Soup.

MINTED LETTUCE SOUP

This is a delicate soup, so take care not to add too much salt or pepper, or to overcook it. It is best made with crisp lettuces, such as Webb or Cos, and as only the outer leaves are used, the young hearts can be used in a salad.

15g ($\frac{1}{2}$oz) butter
1 large onion, peeled and chopped
2 large lettuces, outside leaves only
5–6 fresh sorrel or spinach leaves, chopped
  (optional)
3 medium potatoes, peeled and cubed
600ml (1 pint) chicken or vegetable stock or
  water
600ml (1 pint) milk
salt
freshly ground black pepper
1 egg yolk
2 tablespoons single cream or top of the milk
4–5 fresh mint leaves, chopped, or 1 teaspoon
  dried mint
finely chopped fresh mint, to garnish
croûtons, to serve

Preparation time: 10–15 minutes
Cooking time: 30–35 minutes

1. Melt the butter in a saucepan, add the onion and fry until translucent. Add the lettuce and sorrel or spinach leaves, if used, cover and cook gently for a further 5 minutes.
2. Stir in the potatoes, stock or water, milk, and salt and pepper to taste, and bring to the boil. Cover and simmer for 15–20 minutes or until the potato is tender.
3. Purée the soup in a blender or food processor, or work through a sieve. Stir the egg yolk and cream or top of the milk together in a cup and, if using a blender, add them to the last batch of soup being puréed. Alternatively, return the soup to the rinsed pan and stir in the yolk and cream or milk mixture.
4. Taste and adjust the seasoning and add the mint. Heat through but do not allow the soup to boil.
5. Serve very hot, garnished with more mint and with croûtons.

Serves 4

Nutrition content per serving Carbohydrate: 20g Fat: 8g
Fibre: 3g Kilocalories: 259

LEFT: Minted Lettuce Soup. ABOVE: Gazpacho Cream.

GAZPACHO CREAM

225g (8oz) tomatoes, skinned and chopped
150g (5oz) cucumber, peeled and chopped
40g (1$\frac{1}{2}$oz) spring onions, finely chopped
50g (2oz) green or red peppers, cored, seeded and
  chopped
1–2 garlic cloves, peeled and crushed
2 tablespoons fresh white breadcrumbs
1$\frac{1}{2}$ tablespoons red wine vinegar
3 tablespoons olive oil
300ml ($\frac{1}{2}$ pint) chicken stock
1 tablespoon chopped fresh basil, or good pinch of
  dried basil
pinch of dried oregano
salt
freshly ground black pepper
5 tablespoons single cream

Preparation time: 30 minutes, plus marinating overnight and chilling

1. Place the tomatoes, cucumber, spring onions and peppers in a bowl with the garlic, breadcrumbs, vinegar, oil and stock. Add half the fresh basil or a good pinch of dried basil, the oregano, and salt and pepper to taste.
2. Cover and leave to marinate overnight in the refrigerator.
3. The next day, purée the soup in a blender or work through a fine vegetable mill. Strain through a sieve and add the cream.
4. Pour the soup into a tureen. Sprinkle with the rest of the fresh basil, or if none is available, chopped parsley. Serve chilled.

Serves 4

Nutrition content per serving Carbohydrate: 6g Fat: 15g
Fibre: 1g Kilocalories: 167

LENTIL POTTAGE

450g (1lb) ham knuckle, soaked overnight
175g (6oz) red lentils
1 large onion, peeled and chopped
1 medium carrot, peeled and thickly sliced
1 medium celery stick, chopped
1.5 litres (2½ pints) water
freshly ground black pepper
1 tablespoon Worcestershire sauce
salt
croûtons, to serve

Preparation time: 10 minutes, plus soaking
Cooking time: about 2 hours

1. Place all the ingredients, except the salt, in a large saucepan and bring slowly to the boil. Skim to remove the froth. Reduce the heat, cover the pan and simmer until the ham is cooked.
2. Remove the knuckle and flake the ham from the bone. Leave the soup to cool slightly, then place the vegetables and liquid in a blender or food processor and blend until smooth.
3. Return to the pan, add the ham and reheat for 5 minutes. Adjust the seasoning, adding salt to taste. Serve with croûtons.

Serves 6

Nutrition content per serving   Carbohydrate: 18g   Fat: 1g
Fibre: 4g   Kilocalories: 115

SOUP OF THE EARTH

25g (1oz) butter
1 large onion, peeled and chopped
100g (4oz) potatoes, peeled and roughly chopped
225g (8oz) carrots, peeled and thickly sliced
225g (8oz) swede, peeled and roughly chopped
900ml (1½ pints) chicken stock
small bunch of parsley
300ml (½ pint) milk
salt
freshly ground black pepper
chopped fresh parsley, to garnish

Preparation time: about 15 minutes
Cooking time: about 30 minutes

1. Melt the butter in a large saucepan, add the onion and fry gently until soft. Add all the other ingredients, except the parsley, milk, salt and pepper, and bring to the boil. Cover the pan and simmer until the vegetables are soft. Leave to cool slightly.
2. Place the vegetables, stock and parsley in a blender or food processor and blend until smooth and the parsley is chopped.
3. Return to the pan, add the milk and reheat. Serve garnished with parsley.

Serves 6

Nutrition content per serving   Carbohydrate: 10g   Fat: 5g
Fibre: 3g   Kilocalories: 97

CURRIED CELERY & APPLE SOUP

450g (1lb) cooking apples, peeled, cored and
    chopped
1 medium onion, peeled and sliced
2 celery sticks, thinly sliced
40g (1½oz) butter
2 teaspoons curry powder (mild or hot, to taste)
1 tablespoon chopped fresh mint
juice of 1 lemon
600ml (1 pint) chicken stock
2 tablespoons semolina
300ml (½ pint) milk
salt
freshly ground black pepper
4 teaspoons sunflower seeds, to garnish

Preparation time: 10 minutes
Cooking time: 35 minutes

1. In a large pan, gently fry the apples, onion and celery in the butter, stirring occasionally, for 5 minutes. Increase the heat to moderate, stir in the curry powder and cook for 3 minutes. Add the mint and lemon juice and pour on the stock, stirring. Bring slowly to the boil, then cover and simmer for 20 minutes, or until the apples are tender.
2. Purée the soup in a blender or food processor. Put the semolina in the rinsed pan and gradually pour on the puréed soup, stirring all the time. Pour on the milk and reheat. Add salt and pepper to taste.
3. Serve the soup hot, or cold, garnished with the sunflower seeds and a sprinkle of curry powder, if liked.

Serves 4

Nutrition content per serving   Carbohydrate: 23g   Fat: 2g
Fibre: 3g   Kilocalories: 129

TOP: Curried Celery & Apple Soup; MIDDLE: Soup of the Earth; BOTTOM: Lentil Pottage.

CREAM OF CAULIFLOWER SOUP

40g (1½oz) butter
1 onion, peeled and finely chopped
450g (1lb) cauliflower, divided into florets
600ml (1 pint) chicken stock
2 teaspoons chopped fresh chervil, or 1 teaspoon
  dried chervil
salt
freshly ground black pepper
600ml (1 pint) milk

Preparation time: 15 minutes
Cooking time: about 40 minutes

1. Melt 25g (1oz) butter in a heavy-based pan, add the onion and fry gently until soft. Add the cauliflower florets, reserving a few tiny sprigs for the garnish. Cook the cauliflower over gentle heat for about 5 minutes, stirring all the time to coat in the butter and onion.
2. Stir in the stock and bring to the boil. Lower the heat, add half the chervil, and salt and pepper to taste, then half cover with a lid. Simmer gently for 20 minutes until the cauliflower is tender, stirring occasionally.
3. Remove from the heat and leave to cool slightly, then purée in a blender or work through a sieve until smooth. Return to the rinsed-out pan and stir in the milk. Bring to just below boiling point, stirring constantly, then simmer gently for about 5 minutes. Check the consistency of the soup, stirring in a little extra milk if it seems too thick.
4. Meanwhile, melt the remaining butter in a separate pan, add the reserved cauliflower sprigs and toss gently in the butter for 1–2 minutes.
5. Taste and adjust the seasoning of the soup, then pour into a warmed tureen or 4 individual bowls. Place a few cauliflower sprigs in each serving, then sprinkle with the remaining chervil. Alternatively, leave a few pieces of chervil whole for garnishing. Serve immediately.

Serves 4

Nutrition content per serving   Carbohydrate: 10g   Fat: 14g
Fibre: 3g   Kilocalories: 192

CARROT & CORIANDER SOUP

40g (1½oz) butter
1 medium onion, peeled and chopped
350g (12oz) carrots, peeled and sliced
1½ tablespoons plain flour
600ml (1 pint) chicken stock
salt
freshly ground black pepper
1½ teaspoons ground coriander
1 bay leaf
1½ teaspoons lemon juice
300ml (½ pint) milk
6 tablespoons single cream
chopped fresh parsley, to garnish

Preparation time: 20 minutes
Cooking time: about 40 minutes

1. Melt the butter in a large saucepan. Add the onion and fry over a gentle heat for about 5 minutes or until soft and lightly coloured. Add the carrots, stir to coat in butter, and fry for a further 2–3 minutes.
2. Stir in the flour and cook for 1–2 minutes, then gradually stir in the stock and bring to the boil.
3. Season well with salt and pepper and add the coriander, bay leaf and lemon juice. Cover the pan and simmer gently for about 30 minutes or until the carrots are very tender.
4. Discard the bay leaf and purée the soup in a food processor or blender, or work through a sieve.
5. Return to a clean pan with the milk and return to the boil. Taste and adjust the seasoning, stir in the cream and reheat gently. Serve at once in warmed soup bowls, garnished with chopped parsley, plus a little freshly ground coriander, if liked.

Serves 4

Nutrition content per serving   Carbohydrate: 18g   Fat: 16g
Fibre: 3g   Kilocalories: 232

TOP: Cream of Cauliflower Soup; BOTTOM: Carrot & Coriander Soup.

Starters

◆

Beginning a meal with a vegetable dish, hot or cold, is an excellent way to stimulate the taste buds: vegetable starters are light and tasty.
They appeal to the eye, too,
with their colour and freshness.
Cold starters are very convenient as they can be made in advance. Globe artichokes served with a cucumber, mint and yogurt dressing are a good choice, as is a garlicky Greek dip based on aubergines that is served with pitta bread, radishes and olives. Or you might like to try an impressive layered vegetable terrine.
When the menu calls for a hot starter, you can choose from deep-fried crumbed mushrooms stuffed with garlic butter or asparagus with a simple yet delicious lime mayonnaise. There is also the popular Chinese starter, crispy fried 'seaweed' – really finely shredded green cabbage.

Crudités with Anchovy Dip (see recipe on page 20).

CRUDITES WITH ANCHOVY DIP

*1 head celery, trimmed, with sticks halved and cut
  into even lengths*
*1 small head purple sprouting broccoli, divided
  into florets*
4 carrots, peeled and cut into thin sticks
1 bunch radishes, trimmed
a few mushrooms, wiped clean
8 asparagus spears, lightly cooked
*1 Golden Delicious apple, cored and cut into
  wedges*
ANCHOVY DIP:
*2 × 50g (2oz) cans anchovies in oil, drained and
  soaked in milk for 20 minutes*
2 tomatoes, skinned, seeded and chopped
2 garlic cloves, peeled and crushed
1 tablespoon tomato purée
2 tablespoons wine vinegar
about 300ml (½ pint) olive oil
fresh dill sprigs, to garnish

Preparation time: about 50 minutes, plus
soaking

1. To prepare the anchovy dip, drain the
anchovies and pat dry with paper towels. Put
the anchovies in a blender or food processor
with the tomatoes, garlic, tomato purée and
wine vinegar. Work to a smooth purée, then
add the oil a drop at a time until the mixture
begins to thicken, as when making mayonnaise.
Continue adding the oil in a thin, steady stream
until a thick, smooth paste is formed, then turn
into a serving bowl. Cover and leave to stand at
room temperature until serving time.
2. To serve, arrange the prepared vegetables in
groups in a large salad bowl or basket, with the
dip placed around in separate serving bowls or
place a bowl of the dip in the centre of a large
tray or platter and arrange the groups of
vegetables around the outside. Garnish with
dill. Serve immediately the vegetables are
prepared or they will lose their crispness.

Serves 4

Nutrition content per serving   Carbohydrate: 10g   Fat: 80g
Fibre: 7g   Kilocalories: 796

CRISPY 'SEAWEED'

You might be surprised or even shocked to
learn that the very popular 'seaweed' served in
Chinese restaurants is, in fact, green cabbage!
Choose fresh, young spring greens with pointed
heads; even the deep green outer leaves of these
are quite tender. This recipe also makes an
ideal garnish for a number of dishes,
particularly cold starters and buffet dishes.

750g (1½–1¾lb) spring greens
oil for deep-frying
1 teaspoon salt
1½ teaspoons caster sugar

Preparation time: 20 minutes, plus drying
Cooking time: 2–3 minutes

1. Wash and dry the spring green leaves, then
shred with a Chinese cleaver or sharp knife into
the thinnest possible shavings. Spread them out
on paper towels or put in a large colander to
dry thoroughly for about 30 minutes.
2. Heat the oil in a wok or deep-fryer, but
before it gets too hot, turn off the heat for
½ minute. Add the spring green shavings in
several batches and turn the heat up to medium
high. Stir with cooking chopsticks and when
the shavings start to float to the surface, scoop
them out gently with a slotted spoon and drain
on paper towels, to remove as much of the oil
as possible.
3. Sprinkle the salt and caster sugar evenly on
top, then mix gently. Serve cold.

Variation: Deep-fry 50g (2oz) split almonds
until crisp and add to the 'seaweed' as a
garnish, to give the dish a new dimension.

Serves 4

Nutrition content per serving   Carbohydrate: 6g   Fat: 20g
Fibre: 6g   Kilocalories: 220

Crispy 'Seaweed'.

TAGLIATELLE WITH WALNUTS

250g (9oz) fresh spinach tagliatelle
salt
100g (4oz) full fat soft cheese
120ml (4fl oz) soured cream
50g (2oz) shelled walnuts, finely chopped
freshly ground black pepper
black grapes, halved and pipped, to garnish

Preparation time: 10 minutes
Cooking time: 10 minutes

1. Cook the tagliatelle in boiling salted water for about 3 minutes, then drain in a colander.
2. Put the soft cheese, soured cream and walnuts into the warm pan and stir over a low heat. Add salt and pepper.
3. When the cheese and cream are beginning to melt, tip in the cooked tagliatelle and shake the pan to coat the pasta thoroughly. Serve immediately, garnished with black grapes.

Serves 3

Nutrition content per serving   Carbohydrate: 62g   Fat: 36g
Fibre: 5g   Kilocalories: 608

AUBERGINE DIP

2 large aubergines, about 450g (1lb) total
1 small onion, peeled and roughly chopped
2 garlic cloves, peeled and roughly chopped
4 tablespoons olive oil
2 tablespoons lemon juice
salt
freshly ground black pepper
TO SERVE:
1–2 tablespoons chopped fresh parsley
black or green olives
radishes
pitta bread

Preparation time: 10 minutes
Cooking time: about 20 minutes

1. Thread the aubergines on to a skewer. Place them on the greased grill of a preheated barbecue and cook for 10 minutes, then turn over and cook for a further 10 minutes.
2. Leave the aubergines until they are cool enough to handle, then peel and chop.
3. Put the aubergine flesh into a blender or food processor with the remaining ingredients and blend until smooth.

4. Transfer the purée to a bowl. Sprinkle with the chopped parsley. Serve with olives, radishes and pitta bread.

Serves 4

Nutrition content per serving   Carbohydrate: 5g   Fat: 15g
Fibre: 3g   Kilocalories: 155

FRIED MUSHROOMS KIEV

24 cup mushrooms
100g (4oz) unsalted butter, softened
2–3 garlic cloves, peeled and crushed
2 tablespoons finely chopped fresh parsley
salt
freshly ground black pepper
2 eggs, beaten
75g (3oz) dried breadcrumbs
vegetable oil, for deep-frying
TO GARNISH:
chicory leaves
parsley sprigs

Preparation time: about 1 hour, plus chilling
Cooking time: about 20 minutes

1. Wipe the mushrooms clean with a damp cloth. Carefully pull out the stalks, keeping the caps whole. Chop the stalks very finely.
2. Put the softened butter in a bowl with the chopped mushroom stalks, garlic, parsley, and salt and pepper to taste. Beat together well. Spoon into the mushroom cavities, then sandwich the mushrooms together in pairs. Use wooden cocktail sticks to secure them.
3. Dip the mushroom pairs one at a time into the beaten egg, then roll in the breadcrumbs. Repeat once more. Chill for 1 hour.
4. Heat the oil in a deep-fat fryer to 190°C (375°F), or until a stale bread cube turns golden in 40–50 seconds. Fry the mushrooms a few at a time for about 5 minutes, turning them frequently with a slotted spoon until golden brown and crisp on all sides. Drain on paper towels and keep hot while frying the remainder.
5. Remove the cocktail sticks and serve immediately, garnished with chicory leaves and parsley sprigs.

Serves 4

Nutrition content per serving   Carbohydrate: 10g   Fat: 36g
Fibre: 4g   Kilocalories: 400

TOP: Tagliatelle with Walnuts; MIDDLE: Aubergine Dip; BOTTOM: Fried Mushrooms Kiev.

COURGETTES A LA GRECQUE

450g (1lb) courgettes
1½ tablespoons salt
150ml (¼ pint) olive oil
150ml (¼ pint) water
1 bay leaf
1 tablespoon chopped fresh thyme
1 teaspoon coriander seeds, crushed
½ teaspoon black peppercorns, crushed
1 tablespoon lemon juice
4 large tomatoes, skinned, seeded and chopped
1 large garlic clove, peeled and finely chopped
chopped fresh thyme, to garnish

Preparation time: 20 minutes, plus draining and chilling
Cooking time: 25–30 minutes

1. Cut each courgette into lengthways slices about 5mm (¼ inch) thick.
2. Put the courgette slices into a colander and sprinkle with the salt; leave to drain for 1 hour. Rinse the courgette slices and pat them dry on paper towels.
3. Put the remaining ingredients into a deep frying pan. Bring to the boil and simmer for 5 minutes.
4. Add the courgette slices to the pan. Cover and simmer gently for about 20 minutes.
5. Transfer to a shallow serving dish; allow to cool and then chill for at least 2 hours before serving, sprinkled with chopped fresh thyme.

Serves 4

Nutrition content per serving   Carbohydrate: 7g   Fat: 38g
Fibre: 1g   Kilocalories: 374

ASPARAGUS WITH LIME MAYONNAISE

225g (8oz) asparagus
2–3 tablespoons mayonnaise
1½–2 teaspoons lime juice
salt
freshly ground black pepper
1 teaspoon grated lime rind
TO GARNISH:
twists of lime
fresh dill

Preparation time: 10 minutes, plus cooling
Cooking time: 5–10 minutes

1. Trim the base of the asparagus, and cook in boiling salted water for 5–10 minutes until the stalks are just tender. Drain well, then leave to cool.
2. Mix together the mayonnaise, lime juice, and salt and pepper to taste.
3. Arrange the cold asparagus on two plates. Put the mayonnaise at the stalk end and sprinkle the lime rind on top of the mayonnaise. Garnish and serve.

Serves 2

Nutrition content per serving   Carbohydrate: 1g   Fat: 14g
Fibre: 2g   Kilocalories: 146

ABOVE: Asparagus with Lime Mayonnaise.
LEFT: Courgettes à la Grecque.

GLOBE ARTICHOKES WITH MINTY YOGURT DRESSING

4 large globe artichokes
3–4 tablespoons lemon juice
salt
1 tablespoon vegetable oil
mint and chervil sprigs, to garnish (optional)
DRESSING:
300ml ($\frac{1}{2}$ pint) Greek yogurt
$\frac{1}{2}$ teaspoon grated lemon rind
1 tablespoon lemon juice
1 tablespoon olive oil
10cm (4 inch) cucumber, peeled, seeded and grated
2 tablespoons chopped fresh mint
2 hard-boiled eggs, finely chopped
2 spring onions, trimmed and finely chopped

Preparation time: 40 minutes
Cooking time: 45 minutes

1. Have ready a bowl of water mixed with 1 tablespoon of the lemon juice. Brush all the cut surfaces of the artichokes with lemon juice as you prepare them, and drop them into the acidulated water. Trim the artichoke stem level with the base of the leaves and, working all round each artichoke, cut off the 2 outside layers of leaves. Cut off the top third of the leaves.
2. Cook the artichokes in a pan of boiling, salted water with 1 tablespoon lemon juice and the oil added, for 35–45 minutes. When they are tender you will easily be able to pull away the outer leaves. Open out the centre of each artichoke, pull out the tight inner ring of pale leaves and, using a teaspoon, scrape out the prickly centre or 'choke'. Wash and drain the artichokes and leave them to cool for about 1 hour.
3. Mix all the ingredients for the dressing. Pour into a small bowl.
4. Serve the artichokes garnished with mint and chervil sprigs, if liked, accompanied by the dressing.

Serves 4

Nutrition content per serving   Carbohydrate: 14g   Fat: 15g
Fibre: 2g   Kilocalories: 226

TOP: Globe Artichokes with Minty Yogurt Dressing;
BOTTOM: Layered Vegetable Terrine.

LAYERED VEGETABLE TERRINE

2 tablespoons olive oil
1 onion, peeled and thinly sliced
350g (12oz) courgettes, sliced
350g (12oz) frozen chopped spinach, thawed
salt
freshly ground black pepper
$\frac{1}{2}$ teaspoon freshly grated nutmeg
225g (8oz) curd cheese
50g (2oz) fresh white breadcrumbs
2 teaspoons chopped fresh basil, or 1 teaspoon dried basil
2 teaspoons chopped fresh marjoram, or 1 teaspoon dried marjoram (optional)
1 egg, beaten
fresh marjoram leaves, to garnish (optional)

Preparation time: about 1 hour, plus chilling
Cooking time: about 1$\frac{3}{4}$ hours
Oven: 160°C, 325°F, Gas Mark 3

1. Heat the oil in a frying pan, add the onion and courgettes and fry gently until soft and lightly coloured. Drain on paper towels.
2. Put the spinach in a heavy-based pan and heat gently until thoroughly dry, stirring frequently. Remove from the heat and stir in salt and pepper to taste and the nutmeg.
3. Work the courgettes and onions to a purée in a blender or vegetable mill, then place in a heavy-based pan and dry out over gentle heat as with the spinach. Transfer to a bowl, then beat in the curd cheese, breadcrumbs, herbs, egg, and salt and pepper to taste.
4. Grease a 450g (1lb) loaf tin liberally with butter and line the base with buttered greaseproof paper. Put half the courgette mixture in the bottom of the tin, pressing it down firmly and levelling the surface. Spread the spinach in an even layer over the top, then press in the remaining courgette mixture.
5. Cover the tin with buttered foil, then stand it in a roasting tin half filled with hot water. Bake in a preheated oven for 1$\frac{1}{4}$ hours or until the mixture feels firm and set.
6. Remove from the tin of water and leave the terrine until completely cold, then chill in the refrigerator overnight until firm.
7. Carefully turn out on to a serving plate and peel off the greaseproof paper. Serve cut into thick slices, garnished with marjoram.

Serves 6

Nutrition content per serving   Carbohydrate: 8g   Fat: 8g
Fibre: 4g   Kilocalories: 145

POTATO SKINS WITH SOURED CREAM DIP

5 large potatoes, scrubbed and dried
150ml (¼ pint) soured cream
1 teaspoon snipped fresh chives
salt
freshly ground black pepper
vegetable oil, for frying

Preparation time: 10 minutes
Cooking time: 1½–1¾ hours
Oven: 190°C, 375°F, Gas Mark 5

1. Prick the potatoes with a fork and bake in a preheated oven for about 1¼ hours until tender; really large potatoes will take about 30 minutes longer.
2. Meanwhile prepare the dip. Mix the soured cream with the chives and salt and pepper to taste. Spoon into a bowl, cover and leave to chill in the refrigerator.
3. When the potatoes are cooked, leave to cool for a few minutes then cut each one into quarters lengthways.
4. Using a teaspoon scoop out most of the potato leaving just a thin layer next to the skin. (Use the scooped-out potato to top a pie.)
5. Pour vegetable oil into a small pan to a depth of 7.5cm (3 inches). There is no need to use a large deep-frying pan.
6. Heat the oil to 180°–190°C (350°–375°F) or until a cube of bread browns in 30 seconds.

7. Fry 4–5 potato skins at a time for about 2 minutes until brown and crisp. Lift from the oil with a slotted spoon and drain on paper towels. Keep the skins hot in the oven while the remaining skins are cooked.
8. Either sprinkle the skins lightly with salt or provide salt for guests to help themselves. Serve with the chilled dip.

Serves 4

Nutrition content per serving   Carbohydrate: 14g   Fat: 23g
Fibre: 1g   Kilocalories: 267

HAZELNUT & CHEESE ROLL

225g (8oz) low-fat soft cheese
75g (3oz) shelled hazelnuts, toasted and chopped
2 celery sticks, finely chopped
1 small green pepper, cored, seeded and finely
*   chopped*
2 spring onions, trimmed and finely chopped
1 medium carrot, peeled and finely grated
3 tablespoons chopped fresh parsley
salt
pinch of cayenne pepper
salad leaves, to serve
COATING:
3 tablespoons chopped fresh parsley
2 tablespoons chopped toasted hazelnuts
2 tablespoons medium oatmeal

Preparation time: 15 minutes, plus chilling

1. In a bowl, mix together the cheese, nuts, celery, chopped green pepper, onions, carrot and 3 tablespoons parsley. Season with salt and cayenne pepper.
2. Beat the mixture well and shape it into a roll about 7.5cm (3 inches) in diameter. Wrap the roll in foil and chill it for 2–3 hours, or overnight.
3. Make the coating. Mix together the parsley, nuts and oatmeal. Roll the cheese mixture in the coating until it is evenly covered.
4. Line a serving dish with the salad leaves. Place the roll on them.

Serves 4

Nutrition content per serving   Carbohydrate: 11g   Fat: 12g
Fibre: 4g   Kilocalories: 200

ABOVE: Potato Skins with Soured Cream Dip.
RIGHT: Hazelnut & Cheese Roll.

Main dishes

◆

A main dish based on vegetables can be made nutritionally complete with the addition of a little meat, cheese, egg or other protein, or can be completely vegetarian if based on pulses and served with rice, bread or another starch. In this chapter you'll find some very tempting ideas for vegetable main dishes both with and without meat.

Stuffed vegetables make super main dishes: here are recipes for peppers filled with rice and mushrooms, courgettes stuffed with a herbed lamb mixture and served with a rich egg and lemon sauce, marrow with a curried beef filling, aubergines stuffed with a rice, ricotta cheese and nut combination, and cabbage leaves rolled around bacon and chestnuts.

You'll also find soufflés, pancakes, pies, pasta, casseroles and curries, and a spicy kedgeree made without any fish!

Black-Eye Pea Casserole (see recipe on page 32).

BLACK-EYE PEA CASSEROLE

225g (8oz) dried black-eye peas, soaked for at least 1 hour
3 tablespoons olive oil
1 large onion, peeled and chopped
2 garlic cloves, peeled and chopped
2 potatoes, peeled and sliced
2 large carrots, peeled and chopped
2 turnips, peeled and diced
2 parsnips, peeled and diced
2 celery sticks, chopped
1 tablespoon chopped fresh parsley
1 tablespoon dried thyme
1 teaspoon dried oregano
2 bay leaves
salt
freshly ground black pepper
1 teaspoon black treacle
2 tablespoons tomato purée
50g (2oz) Cheddar cheese, grated (optional)
fresh herbs, to garnish (optional)

Preparation time: 15 minutes, plus soaking
Cooking time: 2 hours 10 minutes
Oven: 180°C, 350°F, Gas Mark 4

1. Put the black-eye peas and their soaking water into a large saucepan. Bring to the boil and boil for 10 minutes, then cover and simmer gently for 20 minutes.
2. Meanwhile, heat the oil in a flameproof casserole, add the onion and garlic and fry until translucent. Stir in the potatoes, carrots, turnips, parsnips and celery. Cover tightly and cook over a gentle heat for 10 minutes, stirring occasionally to prevent the vegetables sticking.
3. Drain the black-eye peas, which should be almost tender, reserving their cooking liquid. Stir the drained peas into the casserole with the herbs and salt and pepper to taste. Pour over 600ml (1 pint) of the reserved cooking liquid, adding more if necessary so that all the vegetables and peas are covered.
4. Stir in the black treacle and tomato purée. Cover tightly and transfer to a preheated oven. Cook for 1½ hours.
5. Uncover the casserole and discard the bay leaves. Sprinkle with the grated cheese, if used. Cook without a lid for a further 10 minutes. Garnish with fresh herbs, if liked.

Serves 4

Nutrition content per serving   Carbohydrate: 66g   Fat: 17g
Fibre: 20g   Kilocalories: 491

CABBAGE & BACON PIE

1 medium white cabbage, about 1kg (2lb)
salt
3 tablespoons olive oil
225g (8oz) back bacon, rind removed, chopped
1 medium onion, peeled and finely chopped
1–2 garlic cloves, peeled and crushed
2 eggs
150ml (¼ pint) milk
50g (2oz) fresh white breadcrumbs
100g (4oz) Gruyère cheese, grated
freshly ground black pepper

Preparation time: 40 minutes
Cooking time: about 1¼ hours
Oven: 190°C, 375°F, Gas Mark 5

1. Remove 8 large unbroken leaves from the outside of the cabbage. Cook in boiling salted water for 5 minutes. Drain thoroughly.
2. Heat 1 tablespoon oil in a large frying pan, add the bacon and fry over moderate heat until the fat begins to run. Add the onion and garlic and continue frying until the bacon and onion are lightly coloured, stirring constantly. Remove with a slotted spoon and set aside.
3. Chop half the inner leaves from the cabbage. Heat the remaining oil in the pan, add the chopped leaves and fry for a further 5 minutes, stirring frequently
4. Meanwhile, put the eggs in a bowl and beat together lightly with the milk, breadcrumbs, cheese, and salt and pepper to taste. Remove the cabbage mixture from the pan with a slotted spoon and stir into the egg mixture with the bacon and onion.
5. Place 6 drained outer cabbage leaves in the bottom of a well-buttered shallow 1.2 litre (2 pint) baking dish. Overlap them slightly so that they line the dish. Spoon the stuffing mixture into the dish, then fold the leaves over the stuffing. Cover with the remaining 2 cabbage leaves to enclose the stuffing completely.
6. Bake in a preheated oven for 45 minutes or until the filling is set.
7. Remove the cabbage pie from the oven and leave to stand for 5 minutes, then unmould on to a serving platter. Serve hot with sausages.

Serves 4

Nutrition content per serving   Carbohydrate: 25g   Fat: 66g
Fibre: 6g   Kilocalories: 824

Cabbage & Bacon Pie.

VEGETABLE GOULASH

100g (4oz) black beans, soaked overnight
100g (4oz) cannellini beans, soaked overnight
1 tablespoon vegetable oil
100g (4oz) very small onions or shallots, peeled
*   but left whole*
4 celery sticks, sliced into chunks
4 small courgettes, cut into 2.5cm (1 inch) chunks
3 small carrots, peeled and cut lengthways into
*   chunks*
1 × 400g (14oz) can tomatoes
300ml (½ pint) vegetable stock
1 tablespoon paprika
¼ teaspoon caraway seeds
salt
freshly ground black pepper
1 tablespoon cornflour
2 tablespoons water
150ml (¼ pint) soured cream, to serve (optional)
paprika, to garnish

Preparation time: 30 minutes, plus soaking
overnight
Cooking time: 1 hour 20 minutes

1. Drain the beans and rinse them under cold
running water. Put them in two separate pans,
cover with water and bring to the boil. Boil fast
for 10 minutes then lower the heat, half cover
the pans and simmer for about 1 hour until
tender. Drain, rinse and set aside.
2. Heat the oil in a large pan with a lid and fry
the onions, celery, courgettes and carrots
quickly over a high heat until lightly browned.
3. Pour in the tomatoes with their juice and the
stock. Stir in the paprika, caraway seeds, salt
and pepper. Cover the pan and simmer for 20
minutes until the vegetables are tender.
4. Stir both lots of beans into the vegetables.
Blend the cornflour with the water and add to
the pan.
5. Bring to the boil, stirring gently, until the
sauce thickens a little. Cover the pan and
simmer again for about 10 minutes.
6. Spoon the goulash into a warm dish and
serve with soured cream if liked, and a
sprinkling of paprika to garnish.

Serves 4

Nutrition content per serving   Carbohydrate: 38g   Fat: 13g
Fibre: 15g   Kilocalories: 320

TOP: Vegetable Goulash; BOTTOM: Cabbage Rolls with
Bacon & Chestnuts.

CABBAGE ROLLS WITH BACON & CHESTNUTS

For convenience, substitute dried chestnuts for
fresh in this recipe. Pour boiling water over
them and leave to soak overnight. Simmer in
stock or water for 1½–2 hours or until tender,
then drain and use as for fresh.

450g (1lb) chestnuts
1 large firm green cabbage
5 streaky bacon rashers, rind removed, quartered
salt
freshly ground black pepper
25g (1oz) butter, cut into pieces
about 300ml (½ pint) stock or water

Preparation time: 40 minutes
Cooking time: 50–55 minutes
Oven: 180°C, 350°F, Gas Mark 4

1. Place the chestnuts on a chopping board and
with a sharp knife make a cut from just above
the middle down to the pointed end. Cook the
chestnuts in boiling water for 10–15 minutes.
Remove the chestnuts individually and,
protecting your fingers with a cloth or oven
glove, peel the shell away with a knife. The
chestnuts can still be used if they break into
pieces. If the skin does not come away easily,
return the chestnuts to the boiling water for a
few more minutes.
2. Blanch the cabbage in boiling water for 5
minutes. Drain and, if possible, strip away
whole leaves without splitting them.
3. Lay each cabbage leaf on the chopping board
and place a piece of bacon and 1–2 chestnuts in
each. Use two leaves together if they are very
delicate. Roll up each leaf into a parcel and
place, with the overlapping edge underneath, in
a well greased shallow ovenproof dish. Pack the
parcels in tightly, in one layer if possible. Any
leftover whole chestnuts can be pressed in
between the parcels.
4. Sprinkle with a little salt and pepper and add
the butter. Pour in enough of the stock or water
to come 5mm (¼ inch) up the parcels. Cover
with a lid or foil, and cook in a preheated oven
for 25 minutes. Uncover and cook for a further
10 minutes.
5. Serve with the pan juices and garnished with
extra crispy bacon, if liked.

Serves 4

Nutrition content per serving   Carbohydrate: 41g   Fat: 18g
Fibre: 14g   Kilocalories: 358

COURGETTES WITH LEMON SAUCE

8 large plump courgettes
1 small onion, peeled and finely chopped
6 tablespoons olive oil
350g (12oz) finely minced lean lamb or beef
1 tablespoon chopped fresh oregano, or
*   1 teaspoon dried oregano*
2 tablespoons chopped fresh parsley
salt
freshly ground black pepper
4 tablespoons cooked rice
EGG AND LEMON SAUCE:
3 egg yolks
1 tablespoon water
6 tablespoons lemon juice

Preparation time: about 30 minutes
Cooking time: 45–50 minutes
Oven: 190°C, 375°F, Gas Mark 5

1. Top and tail each courgette. Using an apple corer or small sharp knife, 'tunnel through' each courgette, leaving an outer shell about 5mm (¼ inch) thick.
2. Gently fry the onion in 2 tablespoons of the olive oil for 2 minutes. Add the minced meat and fry until lightly browned.
3. Mix the fried meat and onion with the oregano, parsley, salt and pepper to taste, and the cooked rice.
4. Pack each hollowed courgette tightly with the meat mixture. Arrange the stuffed courgettes in an oblong ovenproof dish and spoon the remaining oil over.
5. Bake the courgettes, uncovered, in a preheated oven for 35–40 minutes, until tender.

6. Meanwhile for the sauce, beat the egg yolks with the water, then beat in the lemon juice.
7. Once the courgettes are cooked, remove them carefully with a slotted spoon and place on a serving dish. Whisk the egg yolk mixture into the hot cooking juices in the ovenproof dish. When the sauce thickens, spoon it over the courgettes and serve.

Serves 4

Nutrition content per serving   Carbohydrate: 13g   Fat: 31g
Fibre: 1g   Kilocalories: 417

SPINACH SOUFFLE

155g (5½oz) frozen leaf spinach
50g (2oz) butter
½ onion, peeled and finely chopped
salt
freshly ground black pepper
25g (1oz) plain flour
150ml (¼ pint) milk
3 eggs, separated
½ teaspoon dried thyme
25g (1oz) Cheddar cheese, finely grated

Preparation time: 15 minutes
Cooking time: 1–1¼ hours
Oven: 180°C, 350°F, Gas Mark 4

1. Grease a 15cm (6 inch) soufflé dish.
2. Heat the frozen spinach over a low heat and add 15g (½oz) of the butter. Stir in the onion and season well. Leave to cook gently.
3. Melt the remaining butter in another pan and add the flour. Cook for a few minutes. Allow to cool slightly before adding the milk gradually. Bring to the boil, stirring, and simmer until thickened. Cook for a further 3 minutes. Allow to cool, then add the egg yolks, beating in well. Stir in the thyme and cheese.
4. Stir the sauce into the spinach mixture. Whisk the egg whites until just holding their shape. Fold into the spinach mixture using a metal spoon. Spoon into the soufflé dish.
5. Bake in a preheated oven for 45–50 minutes until risen and golden brown. Serve immediately.

Serves 4

Nutrition content per serving   Carbohydrate: 8g   Fat: 23g
Fibre: 3g   Kilocalories: 300

LEFT: Courgettes with Lemon Sauce.
RIGHT: Spinach Soufflé.

COURGETTE MOUSSAKA

750g (1½lb) courgettes, thinly sliced
120ml (4fl oz) olive oil
1 large onion, peeled and thinly sliced
2 green peppers, cored, seeded and sliced
1 garlic clove, peeled and crushed
450g (1lb) tomatoes, skinned and sliced
1 tablespoon tomato purée
1 tablespoon chopped fresh mint
salt
freshly ground black pepper
100g (4oz) Gruyère cheese, thinly sliced
2 tablespoons plain flour
300ml (½ pint) plain unsweetened yogurt
2 egg yolks
75g (3oz) Cheddar cheese, grated

Preparation time: 20 minutes
Cooking time: 50 minutes
Oven: 200°C, 400°F, Gas Mark 6

1. Fry the courgette slices a few at a time in the oil over moderate heat. Turn them to brown evenly on both sides. Set aside on paper towels while you fry the remainder.
2. Fry the onion, peppers and garlic in the pan for about 4 minutes, stirring once or twice. Add a little more oil if necessary.
3. Stir in the tomatoes, tomato purée, mint, and salt and pepper to taste. Cook for a further 2 minutes.
4. Arrange a layer of courgettes in a greased shallow baking dish. Cover with half the tomato mixture, then with the sliced cheese. Make a layer of the remaining tomato mixture, and cover with the remaining courgette slices.
5. Mix together the flour, yogurt, egg yolks, grated cheese, and salt and pepper to taste. Pour over the courgettes.
6. Stand the dish on a baking sheet and cook in a preheated oven for 25 minutes, until the top is deep brown. Serve hot.

Serves 4

Nutrition content per serving   Carbohydrate: 17g   Fat: 49g
Fibre: 4g   Kilocalories 576

TOP: Courgette Moussaka; BOTTOM: Tomato Tagliatelle with Vegetable Sauce.

TOMATO TAGLIATELLE WITH VEGETABLE SAUCE

Delicatessens and other specialist food shops sell fresh yellow (plain egg) pasta, green pasta, which is coloured with spinach, and red, which has had tomato purée added.

450g (1lb) fresh red tagliatelle
salt
2 tablespoons vegetable oil
15g (½oz) butter
2 medium onions, peeled and sliced
2 garlic cloves, peeled and crushed
450g (1lb) courgettes, trimmed and thinly sliced
1 green pepper, cored, seeded and thinly sliced
2 large tomatoes, skinned and chopped
225g (8oz) button mushrooms, sliced
freshly ground black pepper
2 tablespoons chopped fresh parsley
TOPPING:
150g (5oz) cottage cheese, sieved
25g (1oz) Cheddar cheese, grated
2 tablespoons chopped fresh parsley
2 tablespoons plain unsweetened yogurt

Preparation time: 20 minutes
Cooking time: 25 minutes

1. Cook the tagliatelle in a large pan of lightly salted water for about 5 minutes, or until it is just tender but not soft – 'al dente' as the Italians describe it. Drain the pasta, run hot water through it to prevent it from becoming sticky, and drain it again. Return it to the pan and keep it warm.
2. To make the sauce, heat the oil and butter in a saucepan and fry the onions over moderate heat for 3 minutes, stirring once or twice. Add the garlic, courgettes and green pepper and fry for 3 minutes. Add the tomatoes and mushrooms, stir well, cover the pan and simmer for 10 minutes, or until the vegetables are just tender. Season with salt and pepper and stir in the parsley.
3. To make the topping, lightly mix together the cottage cheese, Cheddar, parsley and yogurt, and season with pepper.
4. Turn the tagliatelle into a heated serving dish, pour on the sauce and toss with two spoons to distribute it evenly. Spoon the cheese topping into the centre and serve at once.

Serves 4

Nutrition content per serving   Carbohydrate: 85g   Fat: 22g
Fibre: 9g   Kilocalories: 600

RICOTTA & SPINACH CANNELLONI

225g (8oz) fresh spinach, washed
100g (4oz) ricotta cheese
3 tablespoons grated Parmesan cheese
2 pinches grated nutmeg
1 egg yolk
1 tablespoon chopped fresh mixed herbs, i.e.
  marjoram, chives, parsley, chervil
salt
freshly ground black pepper
6–8 cannelloni tubes, 100g (4oz) total
TOMATO SAUCE:
450g (1lb) ripe tomatoes, skinned and chopped
1 small onion, peeled and chopped
1 celery stick, chopped
1 tablespoon tomato purée
½ teaspoon sugar
salt
freshly ground black pepper

Preparation time: 30 minutes
Cooking time: about 1 hour
Oven: 180°C, 350°F, Gas Mark 4

1. Place the spinach in a saucepan with just the water that clings to it after washing. Cover and cook for 7–10 minutes, shaking the pan occasionally, until the spinach is tender. Drain well and chop finely.
2. Place the spinach in a bowl with the ricotta cheese, 1 tablespoon Parmesan cheese, the nutmeg, egg yolk, herbs, and salt and pepper to taste. Mix well.
3. Carefully fill the cannelloni tubes with the spinach mixture, using a small teaspoon. Place in a buttered shallow ovenproof dish in one layer.
4. Place all the sauce ingredients in a saucepan. Bring to the boil, reduce the heat and cook for 20 minutes. If liked, press through a sieve or purée in a blender or food processor until fairly smooth.
5. Pour the tomato sauce evenly over the cannelloni, ensuring they are all covered. Sprinkle with the remaining Parmesan cheese.
6. Bake in a preheated oven for 35–40 minutes, until the cannelloni are tender (test by piercing with a sharp pointed knife). Serve hot, garnished with fresh herb sprigs or celery leaves, if liked.

Serves 2

Nutrition content per serving   Carbohydrate: 55g   Fat: 13g
Fibre: 5g   Kilocalories: 437

STUFFED PEPPERS

100g (4oz) long-grain brown rice
300ml (½ pint) stock or water
2 tablespoons olive oil
4 large or 8 small green peppers
1 onion, peeled and chopped
1 garlic clove, peeled and chopped
25g (1oz) pine nuts or blanched almonds, chopped
225g (8oz) mushrooms, chopped
½ teaspoon dried oregano
¼ teaspoon dried basil
salt
freshly ground black pepper
1 × 225g (8oz) can tomatoes
1 tablespoon tomato purée
75g (3oz) Cheddar cheese, grated
parsley sprigs, to garnish

Preparation time: 15 minutes
Cooking time: 1¼–1½ hours
Oven: 200°C, 400°F, Gas Mark 6

1. Put the rice in a saucepan with the stock or lightly salted water with a few drops of oil added. Cover tightly and cook gently for 35–40 minutes. Uncover and cook for a further 5–10 minutes or until all liquid is absorbed.
2. Meanwhile, prepare the peppers. Cut off their tops, and take a thin slice off their bases, so that they will stand upright. Scoop out the cores and seeds, then blanch in boiling salted water for 15 minutes. Rinse and drain.
3. Heat the remaining oil in a frying pan, add the onion and fry until translucent. Add the garlic and pine nuts or almonds, and fry for 2 minutes. Stir in the mushrooms, herbs and salt and pepper to taste, and cook for a further 5 minutes. Remove from the heat and stir in the tomatoes and tomato purée.
4. Drain the rice, if necessary, and stir it into the tomato mixture. Use to fill the peppers and place them close together in a greased ovenproof dish. Sprinkle with the cheese.
5. Cover and cook in a preheated oven for 15 minutes. Uncover and cook for a further 10–15 minutes, to allow the cheese to brown. Serve hot, garnished with parsley sprigs.

Serves 4

Nutrition content per serving   Carbohydrate: 26g   Fat: 18g
Fibre: 5g   Kilocalories: 307

TOP: Ricotta & Spinach Cannelloni; BOTTOM: Stuffed Peppers.

SPICED RICE & LENTIL KEDGEREE

225g (8oz) brown continental lentils, soaked and
   drained
3 tablespoons vegetable oil
1 medium onion, peeled and chopped
2 garlic cloves, peeled and finely chopped
1 teaspoon ground cumin
$\frac{1}{2}$ teaspoon ground turmeric
$\frac{1}{2}$ teaspoon ground coriander
large pinch of cayenne pepper
1 tablespoon finely chopped peeled root ginger
225g (8oz) brown rice
1 litre (1$\frac{3}{4}$ pints) chicken stock
salt
freshly ground black pepper
2 tablespoons chopped fresh coriander or parsley
TO SERVE:
1 small onion, peeled and thinly sliced into rings
2 medium bananas, sliced and tossed in 2
   tablespoons lemon juice
2 hard-boiled eggs, quartered
parsley sprigs

Preparation time: 20 minutes, plus soaking
Cooking time: about 55 minutes

1. Cook the lentils in boiling unsalted water for
10 minutes. Drain and set aside.
2. Heat the oil in a large frying pan and fry the
onion over moderate heat for 3 minutes,
stirring once or twice. Stir in the garlic, cumin,
turmeric, coriander, cayenne and ginger and
cook for 1 minute, then stir in the lentils and
rice. Pour on the stock and bring to the boil.
3. Cover the pan and simmer for 45 minutes
until the rice and lentils are tender. Season with
salt and pepper and, if there is any liquid

remaining, boil uncovered for a few minutes.
Stir in the chopped herb.
4. Turn the kedgeree into a heated serving dish.
Scatter the onion rings on top and serve with
bananas and eggs garnished with parsley.

Serves 4

Nutrition content per serving   Carbohydrate: 83g   Fat: 16g
Fibre: 11g   Kilocalories: 546

CHEESE CRUST VEGETABLE PIE

50g (2oz) butter
1 onion, peeled and sliced
3 carrots, peeled and sliced
1 × 200g (7oz) can sweetcorn kernels
50g (2oz) mushrooms, sliced
2 celery sticks, chopped
1 × 50g (2oz) packet leek soup
freshly ground black pepper
CHEESE PASTRY:
175g (6oz) plain flour
pinch of salt
100g (4oz) butter
75g (3oz) Cheddar cheese, finely grated
2–3 tablespoons cold water, to mix
1 egg, beaten, to glaze

Preparation time: 1 hour
Cooking time: 45 minutes
Oven: 200°C, 400°F, Gas Mark 6; then 180°C,
350°F, Gas Mark 4

1. Sift the flour and salt into a mixing bowl.
Rub in the butter and stir in the cheese. Bind
with water. Wrap and chill until needed.
2. For the filling, melt the butter in a pan and
fry the vegetables for a few minutes. Drain on
paper towels. Make up the packet of leek soup
as directed, but using 600ml (1 pint) water
only. Stir in the vegetables, add pepper and
pour into a 750ml (1$\frac{1}{2}$ pint) pie dish.
3. Roll out the pastry to top the pie. Trim and
flute the edges. Use the pastry trimmings to
make leaves to decorate the top. Brush the
pastry with beaten egg and bake in a preheated
oven for 15 minutes, then reduce the heat and
bake for a further 20 minutes. Serve hot.

Serves 4

Nutrition content per serving   Carbohydrate: 54g   Fat: 40g
Fibre: 8g   Kilocalories: 622

ABOVE: Spiced Rice & Lentil Kedgeree.
RIGHT: Cheese Crust Vegetable Pie.

VEGETABLE-CHEESE SOUFFLE

225g (8oz) peeled potatoes
225g (8oz) prepared cauliflower, carrot, swede,
* parsnips or Brussels sprouts (or a mixture)*
4 tablespoons single cream
3 eggs, separated
100g (4oz) cheese, grated
salt
freshly ground black pepper

Preparation time: 30 minutes
Cooking time: 40 minutes
Oven: 220°C, 425°F, Gas Mark 7

1. Cook the potatoes in boiling salted water until tender. At the same time, cook the cauliflower or other vegetable in boiling salted water. Drain all the vegetables well.
2. Mash the potatoes with the other vegetables, then beat in the cream, egg yolks, grated cheese, and salt and pepper.
3. Whisk the egg whites until stiff, then fold into the vegetable mixture. Spoon into a greased 18cm (7 inch) soufflé dish.
4. Bake in a preheated oven for 20 minutes until well risen and lightly coloured on top. Serve immediately.

Serves 4

Nutrition content per serving   Carbohydrate: 16g   Fat: 21g
Fibre: 3g   Kilocalories: 319

MARROW MADRAS

1 tablespoon oil
1 small onion, peeled and finely chopped
1 small dessert apple, peeled, cored and chopped
225g (8oz) minced beef
2 teaspoons curry powder
2 teaspoons plain flour
1 tablespoon tomato purée
salt
1 medium marrow, peeled, halved lengthways and
* seeded*
300ml (½ pint) hot beef stock
fresh herb sprigs, to garnish

Preparation time: 20 minutes
Cooking time: about 1 hour
Oven: 180°C, 350°F, Gas Mark 4

1. Heat the oil in a frying pan. Add the onion and apple and fry until the onion is translucent.

Add the minced beef and continue frying until the beef is evenly browned and crumbly.
2. Stir in the curry powder, flour and tomato purée. Cook until all the excess liquid has evaporated. Season lightly with salt.
3. Divide the beef mixture between the marrow halves and press it in firmly. Arrange the halves side by side in a baking dish and pour the hot stock around them.
4. Cover and cook in a preheated oven for about 45 minutes or until the marrow is tender. Serve hot, with the cooking juices spooned over and a herb garnish, if liked.

Serves 4

Nutrition content per serving   Carbohydrate: 12g   Fat: 7g
Fibre: 4g   Kilocalories: 157

THREE BEAN CURRY

100g (4oz) butter
2 medium onions, peeled and finely chopped
3 garlic cloves, peeled and crushed
1 tablespoon ground coriander
1 teaspoon garam masala powder
1 teaspoon chilli powder
1 × 400g (14oz) can tomatoes, chopped with juice
salt
1 teaspoon sugar
1 × 425g (15oz) can butter beans, drained
1 × 425g (15oz) can kidney beans, drained
1 × 425g (15oz) can cannellini beans, drained
fresh coriander sprigs, to garnish

Preparation time: 25 minutes
Cooking time: 30–35 minutes

1. Heat the butter in a saucepan, add the onions and fry until light golden brown.
2. Add the garlic and fry for a few seconds only, then add the coriander, garam masala and chilli powder and stir-fry for a few seconds.
3. Stir in the tomatoes, salt and sugar. Reduce the heat and cook for 10 minutes.
4. Add the drained beans, stir thoroughly then cover and cook gently until heated through.
5. Serve garnished with the coriander sprigs.

Serves 4

Nutrition content per serving   Carbohydrate: 53g   Fat: 22g
Fibre: 22g   Kilocalories: 485

TOP: Vegetable-Cheese Soufflé; MIDDLE: Marrow Madras; BOTTOM: Three Bean Curry.

BAKED AUBERGINES

4 small aubergines
salt
2 tablespoons vegetable oil, plus extra for brushing
1 small onion, peeled and chopped
1 garlic clove, peeled and crushed
1 red pepper, cored, seeded and chopped
2 courgettes, chopped
2 tablespoons chopped fresh mint
4 tablespoons cooked brown rice
8 black olives, stoned and chopped
4 tablespoons chopped cashew nuts
freshly ground black pepper
75g (3oz) ricotta cheese
6 tablespoons wholemeal breadcrumbs
3 large tomatoes, thinly sliced
½ teaspoon dried oregano

Preparation time: 25 minutes, plus draining
Cooking time: 45 minutes
Oven: 190°C, 375°F, Gas Mark 5

1. Halve the aubergines lengthways and scoop out the flesh, taking care not to pierce the skin. Chop the flesh and put it into a colander. Sprinkle the chopped aubergine and the 'shells' with salt and stand the shells upside down on a plate. Leave to drain for at least 30 minutes. Rinse the aubergine under cold running water and dry the flesh and the shells.
2. Heat the oil in a frying pan and fry the onion over moderate heat for 3 minutes, stirring once or twice. Stir in the garlic, red pepper, courgettes and chopped aubergine flesh and cook for 5 minutes, stirring frequently. Stir in the mint, rice, olives and nuts and cook for 2–3 minutes. Season with salt and pepper.
3. Spoon the vegetable mixture into the aubergine shells and place them in a shallow, greased baking dish. In a small bowl, mix the cheese and breadcrumbs with a fork. Sprinkle the topping over the aubergines, arrange the tomato slices on top, brush them with oil and sprinkle with the oregano.
4. Bake the aubergines in a preheated oven for 20–25 minutes, until the cheese topping is crisp and brown. Serve hot or cold.

Serves 4

Nutrition content per serving   Carbohydrate: 21g   Fat: 17g
Fibre: 7g   Kilocalories: 266

TOMATO STUFFED PANCAKES

BATTER:
100g (4oz) plain flour, sifted
¼ teaspoon salt
1 egg, beaten
300ml (½ pint) milk
oil for frying
FILLING:
25g (1oz) butter
½ onion, peeled and finely chopped
4 tomatoes, skinned and roughly chopped
100g (4oz) mushrooms, chopped
1 teaspoon mixed herbs
25g (1oz) fresh white breadcrumbs
salt
freshly ground black pepper
TOPPING:
40g (1½oz) butter
40g (1½oz) plain flour
300ml (½ pint) milk
75g (3oz) Cheddar cheese, grated

Preparation time: 45 minutes
Cooking time: 1½ hours
Oven: 190°C, 375°F, Gas Mark 5

1. Put the flour and salt in a bowl. Add the beaten egg and half the milk. Beat until smooth. Stir in the rest of the milk.
2. Make 8 pancakes in an 18–20cm (7–8 inch) frying pan, and set aside.
3. For the filling, melt the butter and fry the onion, tomatoes and mushrooms until reduced to a pulp. Stir in the herbs and breadcrumbs, and season well.
4. Divide the filling between the pancakes and roll them up. Arrange side by side in an ovenproof dish.
5. To make the sauce, melt the butter in a heavy saucepan, remove from the heat and stir in the flour. Gradually stir in the milk, then return to the heat and bring to the boil, stirring constantly. Simmer for 3–4 minutes, stirring. Stir 50g (2oz) cheese into the white sauce, season and pour over the pancakes. Sprinkle over the remaining cheese.
6. Bake in a preheated oven for 30 minutes.

Serves 4

Nutrition content per serving   Carbohydrate: 40g   Fat: 32g
Fibre: 3g   Kilocalories: 500

TOP: Baked Aubergines; BOTTOM: Tomato Stuffed Pancakes.

Light dishes

◆

& SNACKS

If you're looking for an idea for a dish that's not too substantial, to serve for lunch or a light supper, or for a snack, you'll find it here. There are some mouth-watering recipes for quiches – filled with soft cheese and spicy watercress, with mushrooms, onion and Cheddar, with tomatoes, herbs, anchovies and olives, and with a creamy leek custard.

You might like to try a pie made with crisp leaves of phyllo pastry, filled with spinach and herbs, or a pizza topped with mushrooms, Parma ham, olives, artichoke hearts and mozzarella cheese. If you fancy an omelette, there's a thick, flat version here, filled with vegetables, that can be served hot or cold. You'll also find stuffed baked potatoes, pastries filled with leek and eggs or onions, and Middle Eastern fritters served in pitta bread with salad.

Four Seasons Pizza (see recipe on page 50).

FOUR SEASONS PIZZA

15g ($\frac{1}{2}$oz) dried yeast
300ml ($\frac{1}{2}$ pint) tepid water
450g (1lb) plain flour
$\frac{1}{4}$ teaspoon salt
TOPPING:
5–6 tablespoons olive oil
50g (2oz) button mushrooms, sliced
50g (2oz) Parma ham, cut into strips
3–6 black olives, stoned
4 canned artichoke hearts, thinly sliced
50g (2oz) mozzarella cheese, sliced
1 tomato, skinned and sliced
salt
freshly ground black pepper

Preparation time: 1 hour, plus rising
Cooking time: 30 minutes
Oven: 230°C, 450°F, Gas Mark 8; then 190°C, 375°F, Gas Mark 5

1. For the pizza dough, sprinkle the yeast over half the water, stir and leave in a warm place for 10 minutes until frothy. Sift the flour and salt into a bowl, make a well in the centre and add the yeast liquid and remaining water. Mix to a dough, then knead on a floured surface until smooth and elastic. Shape into a ball, put into a floured bowl and cover with a damp cloth. Leave to rise in a warm place until doubled in bulk – 1–1$\frac{1}{2}$ hours.
2. To make the topping, heat 3 tablespoons olive oil in a pan and gently fry the sliced mushrooms for 5 minutes.
3. Knock back the dough and roll out to a 1cm ($\frac{1}{2}$ inch) thick round on a floured work surface. Transfer to a greased baking sheet and press out to a 30–35cm (12–14 inch) round no more than 5mm ($\frac{1}{4}$ inch) thick. Pinch up the edges all round. Brush the surface of the pizza base with oil and mark gently into four equal sections. Place the fried mushrooms over one section of pizza; the ham and olives over a second section; the artichoke hearts over the third section; and the mozzarella and tomato over the fourth.
4. Season the pizza topping with salt and pepper and sprinkle generously with olive oil. Bake in a preheated oven for 15 minutes. Reduce the oven temperature and bake for a further 10 minutes. Serve cut into wedges.

Serves 4

Nutrition content per serving   Carbohydrate: 92g   Fat: 28g
Fibre: 5g   Kilocalories: 668

LENTIL & WATERCRESS PATTIES

1 large onion, peeled and finely chopped
1 garlic clove, peeled and crushed
3 tablespoons vegetable oil
225g (8oz) split red lentils
600ml (1 pint) chicken stock
few parsley stalks
2 tablespoons tomato purée
100g (4oz) blanched almonds, chopped
1 bunch watercress sprigs, finely chopped
1 tablespoon chopped fresh mint
salt
freshly ground black pepper
2 tablespoons plain flour
oil for frying

Preparation time: 30 minutes
Cooking time: 50 minutes

1. Fry the onion and garlic in the oil over moderate heat for 2 minutes, stirring once or twice. Add the lentils and stir to coat them with oil.
2. Pour on the stock, add the parsley stalks and bring to the boil. Lower the heat, cover the pan and simmer for 40 minutes. The lentils should be soft and have absorbed the stock. If there is still some liquid, increase the heat to evaporate it. Discard the parsley and remove the pan from the heat.
3. Beat the lentils with a wooden spoon and beat in the tomato purée, almonds, watercress and mint. Add salt and pepper to taste.
4. Divide the mixture into 12 and mould into flat 'burger' shapes. Toss them in the flour to coat them thoroughly.
5. Fry the patties in hot oil over moderate heat for about 5 minutes on each side, or until they are crisp. Serve hot or cold.

Serves 6

Nutrition content per serving   Carbohydrate: 27g   Fat: 30g
Fibre: 8g   Kilocalories: 423

Lentil & Watercress Patties.

LEEK & EGG PUFFS

225g (8oz) puff pastry, thawed if frozen
beaten egg, to glaze
2 hard-boiled eggs, shelled and halved lengthways
FILLING:
1 medium leek, about 200g (7oz), sliced
salt
1 tablespoon vegetable oil
1 small onion, peeled and thinly sliced
½ teaspoon coriander seeds, crushed
freshly ground black pepper
50g (2oz) mature Cheddar cheese, cut into small
  cubes

Preparation time: 30 minutes
Cooking time: 30 minutes
Oven: 220°C, 425°F, Gas Mark 7

1. Cook the sliced leek in boiling salted water for 6 minutes, then drain and set aside.
2. Heat the oil in a small pan and fry the onion until golden brown. Add the coriander and salt and pepper to taste, then stir in the cooked leek. Allow the mixture to cool slightly, and stir in the cheese.
3. Roll out the pastry thinly and trim to a 30cm (12 inch) square. Cut it into four 10cm (4 inch) squares. Cut the trimmings into leaf shapes to decorate the puffs. Brush the edges of each pastry square with beaten egg.
4. Divide the filling between the squares, placing it just off centre, and top with half a boiled egg. Fold the pastry over to make a triangle. Seal the edges firmly and brush the tops with beaten egg. Arrange the pastry leaves on top and brush with beaten egg.
5. Bake in a preheated oven for 15–20 minutes until puffed up and golden brown. Serve hot.

Makes 4

Nutrition content per serving   Carbohydrate: 24g   Fat: 29g
Fibre: 3g   Kilocalories: 390

LITTLE LEEK QUICHES

PASTRY:
450g (1lb) plain flour
pinch of salt
350g (12oz) butter
2 egg yolks
3 tablespoons water
FILLING:
50g (2oz) butter
5 large leeks, sliced
1 teaspoon dried oregano
5 eggs
300ml (½ pint) single cream
salt
freshly ground pepper
1 tablespoon chopped fresh parsley
fresh oregano, to garnish (optional)

Preparation time: 45 minutes, plus chilling
Cooking time: 50 minutes
Oven: 180°C, 350°F, Gas Mark 4

1. For the pastry, sift the flour and salt into a mixing bowl and rub in the butter until the mixture resembles breadcrumbs. Bind with the egg yolks and water, then wrap and chill for 20 minutes.
2. Roll out the pastry dough and use to line eight 11.5cm (4½ inch) diameter flan rings placed on baking sheets. Line the pastry cases with greaseproof paper and weigh down with baking beans. Bake in a preheated oven for 15 minutes, then remove the paper and beans and bake for a further 5 minutes. Allow to cool.
3. Melt the butter in a frying pan. Add the leeks and fry gently until translucent. Remove from the heat and allow to cool. Sprinkle over the oregano and divide between the pastry shells. Beat together the eggs, cream and salt and pepper to taste and pour over the leeks. Sprinkle with the chopped parsley.
4. Bake in a preheated oven for 20 minutes. Allow to cool before serving, garnished with fresh oregano, if available.

Makes 8

Nutrition content per serving   Carbohydrate: 51g   Fat: 55g
Fibre: 4g   Kilocalories: 735

TOP: Leek & Egg Puffs; BOTTOM: Little Leek Quiches.

POTATO HERB SCONES

350g (12oz) potatoes, peeled
salt
freshly ground black pepper
2 tablespoons snipped fresh chives
2 tablespoons chopped fresh parsley
75g (3oz) plain or wholewheat flour
a little milk (optional)
oil for frying

Preparation time: 15 minutes
Cooking time: 35 minutes

1. Cook the potatoes in lightly salted boiling water for 15–20 minutes until tender. Drain.
2. Mash the potatoes. Season with salt and pepper and stir in the chives and parsley. Beat in the flour. Add milk if the mixture is dry.
3. Form the mixture into a ball and knead lightly until it is smooth and free from cracks. Roll it out on a lightly floured board to a thickness of 5mm ($\frac{1}{4}$ inch). Prick the surface all over with a fork and cut into neat triangles.
4. Lightly oil a heavy frying pan, heat and cook the triangles, a few at a time, for 2–3 minutes on each side until golden brown.

Makes about 8

Nutrition content per scone   Carbohydrate: 14g   Fat: 2g
Fibre: 2g   Kilocalories: 76

MUSHROOM & ONION QUICHE

225g (8oz) shortcrust pastry (see page 58)
15g ($\frac{1}{2}$oz) butter
1 large onion, peeled and thinly sliced
150ml ($\frac{1}{4}$ pint) milk or single cream
2 eggs
$\frac{1}{4}$ teaspoon salt
freshly ground black pepper
100g (4oz) button mushrooms
50g (2oz) Cheddar cheese, grated

Preparation time: 15 minutes
Cooking time: about 25 minutes
Oven: 200°C, 400°F, Gas Mark 6

1. Roll out the pastry and line a 20cm (8 inch) flan ring on a baking sheet or a flan dish.
2. Melt the butter in a frying pan, add the onion and cook gently until soft but not brown. Cool slightly and place in the pastry case.
3. Lightly beat together the milk, eggs, and salt

and pepper to taste. Reserve 3 mushrooms and finely chop the rest. Add to the egg mixture and pour into the pastry case. Thinly slice the reserved mushrooms and scatter on top. Sprinkle with the cheese.
4. Bake in a preheated oven for 25 minutes until the pastry is cooked and the filling set.

Serves 4

Nutrition content per serving   Carbohydrate: 30g   Fat: 27g
Fibre: 2g   Kilocalories: 408

PISSALADIERE

2 tablespoons olive oil
2 large onions, peeled and sliced
1 garlic clove, peeled and crushed
1 × 225g (8oz) can tomatoes, drained and
   chopped
1 tablespoon tomato purée
$\frac{1}{2}$ teaspoon dried basil
1 teaspoon sugar
salt
freshly ground black pepper
225g (8oz) shortcrust pastry (see page 58)
4 tomatoes, skinned and thinly sliced
50g (2oz) Gruyère or Cheddar cheese, grated
1 × 50g (2oz) can anchovies in olive oil, drained
25g (1oz) black olives, stoned and halved

Preparation time: 1 hour, plus resting
Cooking time: 40–45 minutes
Oven: 190°C, 375°F, Gas Mark 5

1. Heat the oil in a frying pan. Add the onions and garlic and fry until golden. Stir in the canned tomatoes, tomato purée, basil, sugar, salt and pepper. Bring to the boil. Set aside.
2. Roll out the pastry and use to line a 20cm (8 inch) flan dish or ring placed on a baking sheet.
3. Spread the tomato mixture in the pastry case. Arrange tomato slices in a circle on top, sprinkle with the cheese then arrange drained anchovies in a lattice pattern on top. Put halved olives in each 'window' of the lattice.
4. Bake in a preheated oven for 25–30 minutes or until the pastry is golden brown. Remove and leave to rest for 10 minutes before serving.

Serves 4

Nutrition content per serving   Carbohydrate: 35g   Fat: 30g
Fibre: 4g   Kilocalories: 444

CLOCKWISE FROM THE TOP: Pissaladière; Mushroom & Onion Quiche; Potato Herb Scones.

SPINACH & PHYLLO PIE

1 large onion, peeled and thinly sliced
8 spring onions, chopped or thinly sliced
6 tablespoons olive oil
100g (4oz) butter, melted
1.25kg (2½lb) fresh spinach, washed and shredded
salt
freshly ground black pepper
6 tablespoons chopped fresh parsley
4 teaspoons dried dill or oregano
3 eggs, beaten
450g (1lb) phyllo pastry, thawed if frozen

Preparation time: 30–35 minutes
Cooking time: 50–55 minutes
Oven: 190°C, 375°F, Gas Mark 5

1. Gently fry the onions in 4 tablespoons of the oil and 25g (1oz) of the butter until soft.
2. Add the shredded spinach and stir over a moderate heat until evenly coated in fat. Cover and cook gently for 3–4 minutes.
3. Drain off any excess moisture from the spinach. Season with salt and pepper, and mix in the parsley, dill or oregano and eggs.
4. Mix the remaining oil and butter together and use a little to grease a rectangular tin, 35 × 25 × 7.5cm (14 × 10 × 3 inches) deep.
5. Brush a sheet of phyllo pastry with the butter and oil, and press it into the tin. Brush another sheet of pastry and place on top of the first. Continue until you have put in 7 layers of pastry, each brushed with butter and oil.
6. Spread the spinach filling evenly over the layers of phyllo pastry; trim off the edges of the pastry with scissors, allowing a 2.5cm (1 inch) overlap for shrinkage during cooking.
7. Lay another 7 layers of oiled phyllo pastry on top. Do not press the layers down, but trim off any unnecessary overlap.
8. Brush the top layer well with butter and oil. Using a sharp knife mark squares or diamond shapes. Cut through only the top layers of pastry and not through to the spinach filling.
9. Sprinkle with a little cold water. Bake in a preheated oven for 40 minutes until puffed and golden. Let stand for 5 minutes before cutting.

Serves 6

Nutrition content per serving   Carbohydrate: 34g   Fat: 55g
Fibre: 2g   Kilocalories: 664

BACON STUFFED POTATOES

4 large potatoes, scrubbed
225g (8oz) streaky bacon, rind removed, chopped
100g (4oz) button mushrooms, sliced
120ml (4fl oz) soured cream
salt
freshly ground black pepper
2 tablespoons snipped fresh chives
4 streaky bacon rashers, to garnish

Preparation time: 15 minutes
Cooking time: about 1 hour 20 minutes
Oven: 190°C, 375°F, Gas Mark 5

1. Prick the potatoes, then bake in a preheated oven for 1–1¼ hours until tender.
2. Meanwhile, fry the bacon until crisp. Add the mushrooms and cook for a further 5 minutes.
3. Slice the tops off the potatoes and scoop out the soft potato into a bowl. Add the mushroom and bacon mixture, half of the soured cream and salt and pepper to taste. Fold in half of the chives. Pile back high into the potato skins.
4. Return to the oven and bake for a further 5–10 minutes.
5. Meanwhile, pleat the bacon rashers on to a skewer. Place under a preheated hot grill and cook until golden.
6. Remove the potatoes from the oven. Spoon over the remaining soured cream, top with the pleated bacon rashers and sprinkle with chives.

Serves 4

Nutrition content per serving   Carbohydrate: 37g   Fat: 34g
Fibre: 5g   Kilocalories: 510

LEFT: Bacon Stuffed Potatoes.
ABOVE: Spinach & Phyllo Pie.

FELAFEL IN PITTA POCKETS

2 × 400g (14oz) cans chick peas, drained
1 medium onion, peeled and grated
1 garlic clove, peeled and crushed (optional)
1 teaspoon ground cumin
1 teaspoon ground coriander
¼ teaspoon chilli powder
½ teaspoon caraway seeds
salt
freshly ground black pepper
3 tablespoons chopped fresh parsley
1 egg, beaten
75g (3oz) plain or wholemeal flour
vegetable oil, for shallow frying
4 pitta breads, split open
mixed salad, to serve

Preparation time: 20 minutes
Cooking time: 20 minutes

1. Mash the chick peas to a paste using a fork
or potato masher, or in a food processor.
2. Put into a bowl with the onion, garlic,
cumin, coriander, chilli powder, caraway seeds,
and salt and pepper to taste. Mix to a firm
paste, then stir in the chopped parsley.
3. Form the mixture into small balls and pat
them into small flat cakes about 4cm (1½ inches)
across. Dip into beaten egg and then into flour.
4. Shallow fry in oil in batches for about 5
minutes until crisp and brown. Drain on paper
towels and keep hot in the oven while frying
the rest. Put the pitta bread in the oven to
warm before frying the last batch.
5. Fill the pitta breads with felafels and salad.

Serves 4

Nutrition content per serving   Carbohydrate: 29g   Fat: 5g
Fibre: 6g   Kilocalories: 193

CHEESE & WATERCRESS FLAN

175g (6oz) full fat soft cheese
7 tablespoons soured cream
2 eggs, separated
salt
freshly ground black pepper
2 tablespoons chicken stock or water
2 teaspoons powdered gelatine
1 bunch watercress, about 50g (2oz), finely
   chopped
4 spring onions, trimmed and finely chopped
watercress and tarragon sprigs, to garnish
PASTRY:
175g (6oz) plain flour
pinch of salt
75g (3oz) butter
2–3 tablespoons cold water

Preparation time: 55 minutes, plus chilling
Cooking time: 25–30 minutes
Oven: 190°C, 375°F, Gas Mark 5

1. For the pastry, sift the flour and salt into a
mixing bowl and rub in the butter until the
mixture resembles crumbs. Bind with the water
then wrap and chill for 20 minutes.
2. Roll out the pastry and use to line a 20cm (8
inch) fluted loose-bottomed flan tin. Line with
greaseproof paper and baking beans. Place in a
preheated oven and bake 'blind' for 15 minutes.
Remove the paper and beans and continue
baking for 10–15 minutes until lightly golden.
Allow to cool, in the tin, on a wire rack.
3. Beat the cheese with 4 tablespoons soured
cream, the egg yolks, salt and pepper.
4. Place the chicken stock and gelatine in a
small bowl. Stand in a pan of hot water and stir
until the gelatine has dissolved. Beat the
gelatine into the cheese mixture. Leave on one
side until the mixture is on the point of setting.
5. Whisk the egg whites until stiff. Fold into
the cheese mixture, together with the chopped
watercress and spring onions. Spoon the
mixture into the pastry case, smoothing the
surface level. Chill until set.
6. Spread over the remaining soured cream and
sprinkle with watercress and tarragon sprigs.

Serves 4

Nutrition content per serving   Carbohydrate: 36g   Fat: 45g
Fibre: 2g   Kilocalories: 581

ABOVE: Felafel in Pitta Pockets.
RIGHT: Cheese & Watercress Flan.

FRITTATA

This is a thick, flat omelette cooked on both sides in the frying pan. Good hot or cold, it is an excellent way of using up small quantities of left-over vegetables or rice. Other ingredients could be substituted for those suggested here.

25g (1oz) butter
4 eggs, beaten
275g (10oz) fresh spinach, cooked and lightly chopped, or 100g (4oz) frozen spinach, cooked
3 firm tomatoes, skinned and coarsely chopped
100g (4oz) cooked potatoes, diced, or 75g (3oz) cooked brown rice
salt
freshly ground black pepper
1 teaspoon chopped fresh sage, or ¼ teaspoon dried sage
few drops of Tabasco sauce

Preparation time: 15 minutes
Cooking time: 7 minutes

1. Heat half the butter in a large frying pan until sizzling. Pour in the beaten eggs and stir for a few seconds.
2. Allow the eggs to settle in the pan and then distribute the spinach, tomatoes and potatoes or rice evenly over the surface. Sprinkle with salt, pepper, sage and Tabasco sauce. Cook gently for about 4 minutes until the underside is set and golden brown. Gently lift with a fish slice to check.
3. When the underside is done, tip the omelette out upside down on to a large plate. Add the remaining butter to the pan, run it round over the heat to coat the base, then slide the omelette back into the pan and cook the other side for about 3 minutes.
4. Cut into quarters and serve hot or cold.

Serves 2

Nutrition content per serving   Carbohydrate: 14g   Fat: 22g
Fibre: 6g   Kilocalories: 321

SAVOURY ONIONS IN PASTRY

4 large onions, peeled
25g (1oz) butter
6 back bacon rashers, rind removed, chopped
3 tablespoons chopped fresh parsley
4 tablespoons fresh white breadcrumbs
2 eggs, beaten separately
2 tablespoons grated cheese
salt
freshly ground black pepper
450g (1lb) shortcrust pastry (see page 58 – double quantities)

Preparation time: 25 minutes
Cooking time: 50 minutes
Oven: 190°C, 375°F, Gas Mark 5

1. Carefully hollow out the onions, using a grapefruit knife, leaving 'shells' about 1cm (½ inch) thick. Place the onion shells in a pan of boiling water and par-boil for 6 minutes. Drain and set aside.
2. Chop the hollowed centres from the onions finely. Melt the butter in a pan, add the chopped onion and bacon and fry gently for 3 minutes. Mix the fried onion and bacon with the parsley, breadcrumbs, 1 beaten egg, cheese, and salt and pepper to taste.
3. Press the stuffing mixture well into each onion shell.
4. Roll out the pastry and cut out 4 rounds, each 18cm (7 inches) in diameter. Brush the edges of the pastry rounds with some of the remaining beaten egg. Place a stuffed onion in the centre of each pastry round. Pull up the pastry edges around the onion, pinching them together to seal.
5. Place the onions on a greased baking sheet and brush with beaten egg to glaze. Roll out the pastry trimmings and cut some small leaves to decorate. Fix in position and brush with beaten egg.
6. Place in a preheated oven and bake for 40 minutes. Serve with a simple tomato or mushroom sauce.

Serves 4

Nutrition content per serving   Carbohydrate: 67g   Fat: 56g
Fibre: 6g   Kilocalories: 800

TOP: Frittata; BOTTOM: Savoury Onions in Pastry.

Side dishes

◆

Vegetables to be served as accompaniments to a main dish are often an afterthought in planning a menu, but if you want an imaginative side dish, the recipes in this chapter will provide lots of delicious ideas.

There are potatoes in many guises – thinly sliced and baked in stock, mixed with sweetcorn to make spicy fritters, in a fresh-tasting casserole with cucumber, mushrooms and tomatoes, and baked, stuffed and baked again. You'll find colourful pepper kebabs, piquant carrots, tomatoes baked with herbs and cheese, grilled mustard-topped courgettes, a mixed vegetable curry, an Italian rice dish with spinach and herbs, and so much more!

Spinach & Herb Risotto (see recipe on page 64).

SPINACH & HERB RISOTTO

450g (1lb) spinach, fresh or frozen
2 tablespoons olive oil
100g (4oz) butter
1 small onion, peeled and finely chopped
450g (1lb) short-grain Italian rice
1.6 litres (2¾ pints) chicken stock
1 tablespoon chopped fresh oregano, or 1 teaspoon
  dried oregano
1 garlic clove, peeled and crushed
salt
freshly ground black pepper
75g (3oz) Parmesan cheese, grated
lemon wedges, to serve (optional)

Preparation time: 5 minutes
Cooking time: 30–35 minutes

1. Cook the spinach in a pan, without any
additional water, for 5–10 minutes until tender.
Drain the spinach thoroughly and chop finely.
2. Heat the oil and half the butter in a pan and
gently fry the onion for 3 minutes. Add the rice
and stir over a gentle heat for 5 minutes,
making sure that the rice does not colour.
3. Add a cupful of the stock and cook steadily
until the stock has been absorbed. Add another
cup of stock with the chopped spinach, oregano
and garlic. Cook steadily once again until the
stock has been absorbed. Continue adding the
stock in this way until all the stock has been
absorbed and the rice is tender.
4. Add salt and pepper to taste and stir in the
remaining butter and the Parmesan cheese.
Serve immediately, with wedges of lemon, if
liked.

Serves 6
Nutrition content per serving   Carbohydrate: 68g   Fat: 23g
Fibre: 2g   Kilocalories: 511

SCALLOPED POTATOES

1kg (2lb) potatoes, peeled and thinly sliced
1 large onion, peeled and thinly sliced
salt
freshly ground black pepper
150ml (¼ pint) beef stock
25g (1oz) butter, melted

Preparation time: 20 minutes
Cooking time: about 2 hours
Oven: 180°C, 350°F, Gas Mark 4

1. Make layers of the potatoes and onion in a
well-buttered ovenproof dish, seasoning the
layers with salt and pepper.
2. Bring the stock to the boil and pour over the
potatoes, then brush liberally with the melted
butter.
3. Cover with foil and cook in a preheated oven
for 1½ hours. Remove the foil and cook for a
further 30 minutes or until the potatoes are
cooked through and lightly browned.
4. Place under a moderate grill until the
potatoes are well browned and crispy on top.
Serve hot.

Serves 6
Nutrition content per serving   Carbohydrate: 31g   Fat: 4g
Fibre: 4g   Kilocalories: 162

VEGETABLE FAGGOTS

225g (8oz) carrots, peeled and cut into
  matchstick strips
1 tender celery heart, cut into matchstick strips
4 medium courgettes, cut into matchstick strips
225g (8oz) young French beans, topped, tailed
  and halved
2 small green or red peppers, cored, seeded and
  sliced into 8 thin rings
salt
1 tablespoon lemon juice

Preparation time: 35 minutes
Cooking time: 10 minutes

1. Divide each vegetable into 4 portions – each
person will have a bundle of carrots and celery,
and one of courgettes and beans. Push each
bundle of carrots and celery into a pepper ring
and each bundle of courgettes and beans into a
pepper ring.
2. Fill the base of a steamer with salted water,
add the lemon juice and bring to the boil.
Steam the bundles of carrots and celery for 10
minutes, or until they are just tender, and the
courgettes and beans for about 8 minutes.
Serve immediately.

Serves 4
Nutrition content per serving   Carbohydrate: 10g   Fat: 0g
Fibre: 4g   Kilocalories: 58

TOP: Scalloped Potatoes; BOTTOM: Vegetable Faggots.

CURRIED SWEETCORN & POTATO FRITTERS

50g (2oz) plain or wholemeal flour
½ teaspoon salt
freshly ground black pepper
1 egg, lightly beaten
4 tablespoons milk
1 teaspoon hot curry paste
450g (1lb) potatoes, scrubbed and coarsely grated
1 medium onion, peeled and grated
1 × 200g (7oz) can sweetcorn, drained
4–6 tablespoons vegetable oil

Preparation time: 25 minutes
Cooking time: 25 minutes

1. Put the flour, salt, pepper, egg, milk and curry paste into a large bowl and mix to a smooth, thick batter.
2. Put the grated potato into a clean cloth and twist both ends towards the middle to squeeze out any surplus starchy liquid. This ensures the fritters will be crisp. Pat the potato dry with paper towels and add to the batter with the onion and sweetcorn.
3. Heat 1 tablespoon of oil in a large frying pan and drop the mixture in 1 tablespoon at a time, gently nudging each fritter into a round flat shape with a fish slice. Cook about 4 fritters at a time.
4. Fry the fritters for 3–4 minutes on each side, then drain on paper towels and keep hot while frying the next batch. Alternatively, if time is short, fry the mixture all at once. Divide it between 2 frying pans and make 2 large fritters, increasing the cooking time by about 2 minutes

for each side, and cutting the fritters in half to turn them easily.
5. Put the fritters on a warm dish and serve.

Makes about 20
Nutrition content per fritter   Carbohydrate: 9g   Fat: 4g
Fibre: 1g   Kilocalories: 76

MIXED VEGETABLE CURRY

1 small cauliflower, cut into florets
175g (6oz) carrots, peeled and diced
175g (6oz) potatoes, peeled and diced
salt
225g (8oz) shelled fresh broad beans
1 large onion, peeled and sliced
40g (1½oz) butter
1 tablespoon curry powder (mild or hot, to taste)
1 teaspoon curry paste
1 tablespoon plain flour
2 tablespoons mango chutney sauce
150ml (¼ pint) single cream
2 tablespoons blanched almonds
TO GARNISH:
4 hard-boiled eggs, cut into wedges
fresh coriander sprigs

Preparation time: 45 minutes
Cooking time: 30 minutes

1. Steam the cauliflower, carrots and potatoes over boiling salted water for 10 minutes. Cook the beans in boiling salted water for 5 minutes.
2. Drain the vegetables, reserving the cooking liquid from the broad beans, and keep warm.
3. Fry the onion in the butter over low heat for 5 minutes, then stir in the curry powder and increase the heat to moderate. Fry, stirring, for 1 minute. Stir in the curry paste and flour and cook for 1 minute. Add the chutney sauce.
4. Measure 600ml (1 pint) of the vegetable stock, or make it up to that amount with water or chicken stock. Stir the stock gradually into the curry mixture and bring to the boil. Simmer for 5 minutes, then stir in the cream.
5. Stir in the vegetables and allow them just to heat through. Stir in the almonds. Serve hot, garnished with the egg wedges and coriander.

Serves 6
Nutrition content per serving   Carbohydrate: 17g   Fat: 16g
Fibre: 5g   Kilocalories: 240

ABOVE: Curried Sweetcorn & Potato Fritters.
RIGHT: Mixed Vegetable Curry.

PEAS WITH BACON & ONIONS

25g (1oz) butter
100g (4oz) streaky bacon rashers, rind removed,
    cut into strips
1 bunch spring onions, trimmed and left whole
450g (1lb) shelled fresh peas
4–5 lettuce leaves, coarsely shredded if large
¼ teaspoon sugar
salt
freshly ground black pepper

Preparation time: 10 minutes
Cooking time: 30 minutes

1. Melt the butter in a pan, add the bacon and cook until crisp. Add the onions and cook for a few seconds, then mix in the peas and lettuce.
2. Just cover the peas with water and add the sugar and salt and pepper to taste. Cover and simmer gently for 20–25 minutes until the vegetables are tender. Adjust the seasoning.
3. Drain and turn into a hot serving dish.

Serves 4

Nutrition content per serving   Carbohydrate: 15g   Fat: 14g
Fibre: 7g   Kilocalories: 218

ITALIAN TOMATOES

4 large tomatoes, halved
2 tablespoons oil
1 medium onion, peeled and finely chopped
2 garlic cloves, peeled and crushed
3–4 tablespoons fresh white breadcrumbs
1–2 tablespoons chopped fresh basil or parsley
salt
freshly ground black pepper
50g (2oz) Gruyère cheese, grated
chopped parsley, to garnish

Preparation time: 15 minutes
Cooking time: 15 minutes
Oven: 200°C, 400°F, Gas Mark 6

1. Scoop a little flesh from the centre of each tomato half.
2. Heat the oil in a pan, add the onion and garlic and cook until soft. Add the breadcrumbs, basil or parsley, and salt and pepper to taste. Pile on top of each tomato half and cover with grated cheese. Place in an ovenproof dish.
3. Bake in a preheated oven for 10–15 minutes

until the tomatoes are just cooked and the cheese brown. Garnish with chopped parsley.

Serves 4

Nutrition content per serving   Carbohydrate: 7g   Fat: 12g
Fibre: 2g   Kilocalories: 153

LEMON-GLAZED CARROTS

750g (1½lb) new carrots, lightly scraped
juice of ½ lemon
½ teaspoon demerara sugar
25g (1oz) butter
carrot tops or chopped parsley, to garnish

Preparation time: 5 minutes
Cooking time: about 20 minutes

1. Put the carrots in a saucepan and pour over the lemon juice and just enough boiling water to cover. Add the sugar and half of the butter, cover tightly and simmer until the carrots are nearly tender.
2. Remove the lid and allow the liquid to evaporate completely. Turn into a warmed serving dish, top with remaining butter and garnish with carrot tops or parsley.

Serves 4

Nutrition content per serving   Carbohydrate: 11g   Fat: 6g
Fibre: 6g   Kilocalories: 101

GRILLED COURGETTES WITH MUSTARD

450g (1lb) courgettes, cut in half lengthways
25g (1oz) butter, melted
1 tablespoon Meaux mustard

Preparation time: 10 minutes
Cooking time: about 10 minutes

1. Brush the courgettes with the melted butter and place them, cut side down, on a heated grill pan. Grill under high heat until lightly brown.
2. Turn them over and spread with the mustard. Grill until golden.

Serves 4

Nutrition content per serving   Carbohydrate: 5g   Fat: 6g
Fibre: 2g   Kilocalories: 84

FROM TOP TO BOTTOM: Peas with Bacon & Onions; Italian Tomatoes; Lemon-Glazed Carrots; Grilled Courgettes with Mustard.

FRENCH BEANS IN GARLIC CREAM

450g (1lb) French beans, trimmed and cut in half
salt
225ml (8fl oz) double cream
3 garlic cloves, peeled and crushed
white pepper
fresh chervil or parsley sprigs, to garnish

Preparation time: 10 minutes
Cooking time: 20–25 minutes

1. Cook the beans in boiling, salted water for 10–15 minutes until just tender. Drain well.
2. Meanwhile, place the cream and garlic in a saucepan and boil for 7 minutes to thicken.
3. Add the beans and cook for a further 4–5 minutes. Season, garnish and serve.

Serves 4

Nutrition content per serving   Carbohydrate: 6g   Fat: 12g
Fibre: 3g   Kilocalories: 148

CHEESY BUBBLE & SQUEAK

750g (1½lb) floury potatoes, peeled
little milk
knob of butter
450g (1lb) green cabbage, chopped
1 small onion, peeled and finely chopped
salt
freshly ground black pepper
75g (3oz) Cheddar cheese, grated

Preparation time: 35 minutes
Cooking time: about 1 hour
Oven: 200°C, 400°F, Gas Mark 6

1. Cook the potatoes in boiling salted water until tender; drain. Mash with milk and butter.
2. Plunge the cabbage into boiling salted water and cook for 5 minutes. Drain.
3. Combine the potato and cabbage with the chopped onion and salt and pepper to taste. Spoon into an oiled baking dish, top with the grated cheese and cook in a preheated oven for 30–40 minutes, until browned. Serve hot.

Serves 4

Nutrition content per serving   Carbohydrate: 38g   Fat: 9g
Fibre: 7g   Kilocalories: 273

LEFT: French Beans in Garlic Cream; Cheesy Bubble & Squeak. RIGHT: Skewered Peppers.

SKEWERED PEPPERS

2 green peppers, cored, seeded and cut into
  2.5cm (1 inch) squares
2 medium red peppers, cored, seeded and cut into
  2.5cm (1 inch) squares
2 medium yellow peppers, cored, seeded and cut
  into 2.5cm (1 inch) squares
about 120ml (4fl oz) olive oil
2 garlic cloves, peeled and finely chopped
salt
1 tablespoon crushed black peppercorns
3 tablespoons lemon juice

Preparation time: 15 minutes
Cooking time: 7–10 minutes

1. Thread the peppers on to 8 soaked bamboo skewers. A medium pepper will normally give about 12–16 pieces so there should be about 3–4 pieces of each colour pepper on each skewer. Alternate the colours.
2. Brush the peppers generously on all sides with the oil and cook under a preheated grill for 7–10 minutes, turning and basting with oil every 1–2 minutes. When they are just beginning to char they are done. Baste again with olive oil.
3. Put the skewers on serving plates, then sprinkle each one with a little of the finely chopped garlic, generously season with salt and pepper and then pour over some lemon juice. Serve immediately.

Serves 4

Nutrition content per serving   Carbohydrate: 4g   Fat: 31g
Fibre: 2g   Kilocalories: 299

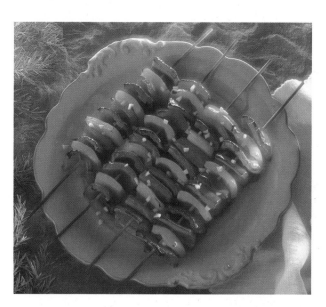

TWICE-BAKED POTATOES

4 large potatoes, scrubbed
1 onion, peeled and finely chopped
50g (2oz) butter, softened
large bunch of fresh parsley, finely chopped
50g (2oz) Cheddar cheese, grated (optional)
salt
freshly ground black pepper

Preparation time: 5–10 minutes
Cooking time: about 1½ hours
Oven: 190°C, 375°F, Gas Mark 5

1. Bake the potatoes in a preheated oven for 1¼ hours, or until they give to the touch.
2. Meanwhile, combine the onion, butter, parsley, cheese, if used, salt and pepper.
3. When the potatoes are cooked, cut them in half lengthways and scoop out the flesh, leaving the skins intact. Mix the cooked potato flesh with the parsley and onion mixture. Pile into the skins, place on a baking sheet and return to the oven to bake for a further 10 minutes or until browned.

Serves 4

Nutrition content per serving   Carbohydrate: 43g   Fat: 15g
Fibre: 5g   Kilocalories: 325

PARSNIP CROQUETTES

450g (1lb) parsnips, peeled and cut into chunks
2 medium potatoes, peeled and halved
salt
50g (2oz) plain flour
25g (1oz) butter, softened
freshly ground black pepper
vegetable oil, for deep frying
parsley sprig, to garnish
COATING:
about 2 tablespoons plain flour
1 large egg, beaten
75g (3oz) dried breadcrumbs
25g (1oz) blanched almonds, finely chopped

Preparation time: 45 minutes, plus chilling
Cooking time: about 35 minutes

1. Cook the parsnips and potatoes in boiling salted water for about 20 minutes until tender. Drain thoroughly, then return to the rinsed-out pan and place over gentle heat to remove excess moisture. Stir constantly to prevent the vegetables catching on the bottom of the pan. Transfer the vegetables to a bowl and leave to cool slightly, then mash until smooth.
2. Beat in the flour, butter, and salt and pepper to taste until evenly mixed. With well-floured hands, form into 8 croquette shapes.
3. Coat with the flour, dip into the beaten egg and then coat with the breadcrumbs mixed with the chopped almonds. Chill for at least 1 hour.
4. Heat the oil in a deep-fat fryer to 190°C (375°F) or until a stale bread cube turns golden in 40–50 seconds. Lower a few of the croquettes carefully into the hot oil, then deep-fry for about 5 minutes until they are golden brown on all sides. Drain on paper towels and keep hot while frying the remainder. Serve immediately, garnished with parsley.

Serves 4

Nutrition content per serving   Carbohydrate: 53g   Fat: 21g
Fibre: 7g   Kilocalories: 421

FENNEL PROVENÇALE

3 fennel bulbs, 450g (1lb) total
50g (2oz) butter
150ml (¼ pint) stock
1 small onion, peeled and finely chopped
½ garlic clove, peeled and crushed
1 × 400g (14oz) can tomatoes
salt
freshly ground black pepper

Preparation time: 20 minutes
Cooking time: 30–40 minutes

1. Cut the fennel bulbs into thin slices, reserving any feathery tops, and place in a bowl. Cover with boiling water and leave to stand for 5 minutes. Drain well.
2. Melt half the butter in a heavy-based pan and add the fennel and stock. Cook gently for 30 minutes or until the fennel is tender.
3. Meanwhile, sauté the onion and garlic in the remaining butter. Add to the fennel along with the tomatoes and seasoning to taste. Cover and cook for 10 more minutes. Serve hot, garnished with the reserved fennel tops.

Serves 4

Nutrition content per serving   Carbohydrate: 4g   Fat: 10g
Fibre: 3g   Kilocalories: 117

TOP: Twice-Baked Potatoes; MIDDLE: Parsnip Croquettes; BOTTOM: Fennel Provençale.

STIR-FRIED VEGETABLES

100g (4oz) fresh bean sprouts
100g (4oz) bamboo shoots
100g (4oz) mange-touts or broccoli
100g (4oz) carrots, peeled
3 tablespoons oil
1 teaspoon salt
1 teaspoon sugar
1 tablespoon stock or water

Preparation time: 15–20 minutes
Cooking time: 3–5 minutes

1. Wash the fresh bean sprouts in cold water and discard the husks and other bits and pieces that float to the surface. It is not necessary to top and tail each sprout.
2. Cut the bamboo shoots, broccoli and carrots into thin slices. If using mange-touts, they need only be topped and tailed.
3. Heat the oil in a preheated wok or frying pan. Put in the bamboo shoots, mange-touts or broccoli and carrots and stir-fry for about 1 minute. Add the bean sprouts with the salt and sugar. Stir-fry for another minute or so, then add some stock or water if necessary. Do not overcook or the vegetables will lose their crunchiness. Serve hot.

Serves 4

Nutrition content per serving   Carbohydrate: 9g   Fat: 11g
Fibre: 3g   Kilocalories: 147

MEXICAN REFRIED BEANS

450g (1lb) dried black-eye, pinto or red kidney
* beans, soaked overnight and drained*
1 medium onion, peeled and diced
1 garlic clove, peeled and crushed
1.2 litres (2 pints) water
100g (4oz) lard or bacon dripping
salt

Preparation time: 5 minutes, plus soaking
Cooking time: about 3½ hours

1. Put the beans in a large pan with the onion, garlic and measured water. Bring to the boil and boil for 10 minutes, then lower the heat and simmer until the beans are tender – about 3 hours. Add more water if necessary.
2. Drain, reserving some of the liquid. Lightly mash the beans with a fork – do not purée.

3. Heat the fat in a wide, heavy frying pan and add the mashed beans. Cook, stirring and turning, until the beans are thickened and the fat is absorbed. Salt to taste. Add a little of the reserved bean liquid if they look dry.

Serves 8

Nutrition content per serving   Carbohydrate: 26g   Fat: 13g
Fibre: 14g   Kilocalories: 267

MIDDLE EASTERN-STYLE KEBABS

1 aubergine, cut into 2.5cm (1 inch) cubes
salt
8 button onions, peeled
2 medium courgettes, cut into 1cm (½ inch) slices
1 red pepper, cored, seeded and cut into cubes
8 cherry tomatoes
150ml (¼ pint) plain unsweetened yogurt
1 garlic clove, peeled and crushed
½ teaspoon ground ginger
3 tablespoons olive oil
freshly ground black pepper

Preparation time: 20 minutes, plus draining and marinating
Cooking time: about 13 minutes

1. Put the aubergine into a colander and sprinkle with salt. Drain for 30 minutes.
2. Simmer the button onions in boiling water for 5 minutes, then drain.
3. Rinse the aubergine cubes and pat dry on paper towels. Thread the aubergine, onions, courgettes, red pepper and tomatoes on to four medium kebab skewers.
4. Mix the yogurt with the garlic, ginger, oil, and salt and pepper to taste.
5. Place the kebabs in a large shallow dish. Spoon over the yogurt mixture and marinate in the refrigerator for 3 hours.
6. Remove the kebabs from the yogurt mixture, shaking gently to allow the excess to drip off. Place the kebabs on the rack of the grill pan. Place under a preheated grill and cook the kebabs for about 4 minutes on each side, brushing with the yogurt mixture during cooking. Serve hot.

Serves 4

Nutrition content per serving   Carbohydrate: 8g   Fat: 12g
Fibre: 3g   Kilocalories: 149

TOP: Stir-Fried Vegetables; MIDDLE: Mexican Refried Beans; BOTTOM: Middle Eastern-Style Kebabs.

SWEDE & ORANGE PURÉE

*1 swede, about 600g (1¼lb), peeled and cut into
   chunks*
4 tablespoons orange juice
salt
freshly ground black pepper
strips of orange rind and parsley sprig, to garnish

Preparation time: 15 minutes
Cooking time: 20–25 minutes

1. Cook the swede in boiling salted water for
15–20 minutes or until tender. Drain well.
2. Put the swede in a food processor, add the
orange juice and process until puréed. Add salt
and pepper to taste.
3. Return the purée to the saucepan, cover and
reheat for 2–3 minutes. Stir again before
serving, garnished with the orange strips and
parsley.

Serves 4

Nutrition content per serving   Carbohydrate: 7g   Fat: 0g
Fibre: 3g   Kilocalories: 33

ONIONS BRAISED IN CIDER WITH SAGE

2 large Spanish onions, about 450g (1lb) total
1 tablespoon vegetable oil
300ml (½ pint) dry cider
*2 teaspoons chopped fresh sage, or ½ teaspoon
   dried sage*
salt
freshly ground black pepper
1 teaspoon cornflour
1 tablespoon water

Preparation time: 15 minutes
Cooking time: 1 hour
Oven: 180°C, 350°F, Gas Mark 4

1. Remove the papery skins from the onions
and cut each into 4. Trim the bases very lightly
so that the quarters stay intact during cooking.
2. Heat the oil in a frying pan and quickly fry
the onion quarters on all sides until golden
brown. Place them in a small shallow casserole,
cut-side up.
3. Pour the cider into the pan and add the sage

and salt and pepper to taste. Bring to the boil,
then pour over the onions.
4. Cover the casserole and cook in a preheated
oven for 40 minutes.
5. Remove from the oven. Blend the cornflour
with the water and stir into the liquor
surrounding the onions. Cover again and return
to the oven to cook for a further 20 minutes, by
which time the onions will be tender and the
sauce slightly thickened. Serve hot.

Serves 4

Nutrition content per serving   Carbohydrate: 9g   Fat: 4g
Fibre: 1g   Kilocalories: 72

STIR-FRIED BROCCOLI

450g (1lb) broccoli or cauliflower
3 tablespoons oil
1 teaspoon salt
1 teaspoon sugar
3 tablespoons stock or water

Preparation time: 10 minutes
Cooking time: $2\frac{1}{2}$–$3\frac{1}{2}$ minutes

1. Cut the broccoli or cauliflower into florets.
Do not discard the stalks; just peel off the
tough skin.
2. Heat the oil in a preheated wok or frying pan
and stir-fry the broccoli or cauliflower for
about 30 seconds. Add the salt, sugar and stock
or water and cook for 2–3 minutes at most,
stirring a few times during cooking. Serve hot.

Serves 4

Nutrition content per serving   Carbohydrate: 3g   Fat: 11g
Fibre: 2g   Kilocalories: 120

TOP: Swede & Orange Purée; MIDDLE: Onions Braised
in Cider with Sage; BOTTOM: Stir-Fried Broccoli.

CUCUMBER, POTATO & MUSHROOM CASSEROLE

40g (1½oz) butter
2 medium onions, peeled and finely chopped
225g (8oz) small new potatoes, scrubbed
150ml (¼ pint) chicken stock
salt
freshly ground black pepper
1 cucumber, peeled and cut into thick slices
175g (6oz) button mushrooms, halved or
  quartered if large
225g (8oz) tomatoes, skinned and quartered
pinch of sugar
chopped fresh parsley or dill, to garnish

Preparation time: 25 minutes
Cooking time: 30 minutes

1. Melt the butter in a heavy-based pan, add the onions and cook gently until soft but not coloured. Cut any large potatoes into cubes, but leave the small ones whole. Add the potatoes, stock, salt and pepper to the pan. Bring to the boil, cover and cook for 10 minutes.
2. Add the cucumber slices and mushrooms. Simmer for another 10 minutes, then add the tomatoes and sugar. Cook for a few more minutes until the vegetables are tender.
3. Pile into a hot deep serving dish and sprinkle with the parsley or dill. Serve hot.

Serves 4

Nutrition content per serving   Carbohydrate: 18g   Fat: 9g
Fibre: 4g   Kilocalories: 159

BRAISED CELERY

25g (1oz) butter
1 onion, peeled and finely chopped
2 medium-sized carrots, peeled and diced
8 celery sticks, cut in half lengthways
300ml (½ pint) chicken stock
salt
freshly ground black pepper
chopped fresh parsley, to garnish

Preparation time: 20 minutes
Cooking time: 1–1¼ hours
Oven: 180°C, 350°F, Gas Mark 4

1. Melt the butter in a frying pan and fry the onion and carrots for a couple of minutes. Add the celery and cook for 2 minutes.

2. Put the vegetables into an ovenproof dish and pour on the stock. Season well with salt and pepper. Cover and cook in a preheated oven for 1–1¼ hours. Serve garnished with chopped parsley.

Serves 4

Nutrition content per serving   Carbohydrate: 6g   Fat: 5g
Fibre: 5g   Kilocalories: 77

LEMON CABBAGE WITH POPPY SEEDS

The contrast provided by the green and white cabbage gives a particularly attractive appearance to this simple vegetable dish.

150ml (¼ pint) water
½ teaspoon salt
350g (12oz) spring greens or green cabbage,
  shredded
350g (12oz) hard white cabbage, shredded
25g (1oz) butter, cut into small pieces
grated rind of 1 lemon
1½ teaspoons poppy seeds
freshly ground black pepper
2–3 tablespoons soured cream, to serve (optional)

Preparation time: 5 minutes
Cooking time: 10 minutes

1. Put the water into a large pan, add the salt and bring to the boil. Add both green and white cabbages, cover and simmer steadily for 7–10 minutes. The cabbage should be crisply tender and most of the water absorbed.
2. Take the lid off the pan and boil quickly to reduce any remaining liquid.
3. Add the pieces of butter, the lemon rind, poppy seeds and lots of black pepper. Stir briefly until the butter is melted and the cabbage well coated.
4. Spoon the hot cabbage into a warm dish and serve with soured cream spooned over the top if liked.

Serves 4

Nutrition content per serving   Carbohydrate: 6g   Fat: 7g
Fibre: 5g   Kilocalories: 106

TOP: Cucumber, Potato & Mushroom Casserole;
MIDDLE: Braised Celery; BOTTOM: Lemon Cabbage
with Poppy Seeds.

Salads

◆

Salads are no longer just warm weather food. At any time of year, a nutritious, fresh-tasting salad is welcome, as a side dish or as a meal in itself. The recipes in this chapter include many ideas for accompanying salads – slices of crunchy fennel and apple with raisins in a soured cream dressing, salad greens dressed with a creamy Roquefort cheese mixture, tiny new potatoes tossed in a piquant dressing made with capers and gherkin, and a delicious mixture of grated carrot, apple, sunflower seeds and cashew nuts.

A main dish salad is an excellent way to use up leftover meat, fish and poultry, and here you'll find some very clever ways to serve roast beef, ham, smoked trout and smoked chicken, as well as canned fish (tuna and sardines) and delicatessen meats such as salami and spicy chorizo sausage.

Smoked Chicken & Fruit Salad (see recipe on page 82).

SMOKED CHICKEN & FRUIT SALAD

1 lettuce, shredded
2 celery sticks, chopped
1 red pepper, cored, seeded and sliced
25g (1oz) walnut halves
75g (3oz) green grapes, peeled, halved and seeded
1 dessert pear, peeled, cored and sliced
225g (8oz) smoked chicken, skinned, boned and
    cut into strips or cubes
DRESSING:
2 tablespoons plain unsweetened yogurt
2 tablespoons mayonnaise
2 tablespoons grated cucumber
1 teaspoon grated onion
$\frac{1}{2}$ teaspoon chopped fresh tarragon
salt
freshly ground black pepper
TO GARNISH:
1 dessert pear, cored and sliced
few fresh tarragon sprigs

Preparation time: 25 minutes

1. In a large salad bowl, mix the lettuce with
the celery, red pepper, walnuts, grapes, pear
and smoked chicken.
2. Mix the yogurt with the mayonnaise,
cucumber, onion and tarragon, blending well.
Add salt and pepper to taste.
3. Just before serving, spoon the dressing over
the salad ingredients and toss well to mix.
4. Garnish with slices of pear and a few sprigs
of fresh tarragon.

Variation: Make the dressing by mixing 2
tablespoons soured cream with 2 tablespoons
mayonnaise, 1 tablespoon grated courgette or
cucumber, 2 teaspoons grated onion,
1 tablespoon chopped roast peanuts and salt
and pepper to taste.

Serves 4 as a main dish

Nutrition content per serving   Carbohydrate: 8g   Fat: 14g
Fibre: 3g   Kilocalories: 228

CHRISTMAS COLESLAW

100g (4oz) red cabbage, finely shredded
100g (4oz) white cabbage, finely shredded
2 dessert apples, preferably red-skinned, cored and
    thinly sliced
50g (2oz) shelled nuts, chopped, e.g. walnuts,
    almonds or hazelnuts
150ml ($\frac{1}{4}$ pint) mayonnaise
2 tablespoons French dressing (see page 85)
fresh parsley leaves, to garnish

Preparation time: 30 minutes

1. Mix together the cabbages, apples and
chopped nuts in a large bowl.
2. Mix the mayonnaise with the French
dressing. Pour over the cabbage salad and toss
until everything is thoroughly coated.
3. Transfer to a serving dish and garnish with
the parsley.

Serves 4 as a side salad

Nutrition content per serving   Carbohydrate: 11g   Fat: 42g
Fibre: 5g   Kilocalories: 432

BEETROOT & ORANGE SALAD

450g (1lb) cooked beetroot, skinned
150ml ($\frac{1}{4}$ pint) soured cream
1 medium orange
2 tablespoons chopped fresh chives
salt
freshly ground black pepper
chopped fresh chives, to garnish

Preparation time: 20 minutes

1. Cut the beetroot into dice about 1cm ($\frac{1}{2}$ inch)
square and arrange in a shallow serving dish.
2. Put the soured cream into a mixing bowl.
Add the grated rind and juice from half the
orange. Cut the peel and pith away from the
remaining orange half and cut the flesh into
segments. Scatter the orange segments over the
beetroot.
3. Mix the chives and salt and pepper to taste
with the soured cream. Pour this dressing over
the beetroot and orange, but do not stir.
Sprinkle with more chives and serve at once.

Serves 4 as a side salad

Nutrition content per serving   Carbohydrate: 14g   Fat: 8g
Fibre: 3g   Kilocalories: 136

TOP: Christmas Coleslaw; BOTTOM: Beetroot &
Orange Salad.

WINTER VEGETABLE SALAD

4 medium waxy potatoes, peeled, cooked and diced
1 large celery stick, finely chopped
2 carrots, peeled and grated
1 small onion, peeled and finely chopped
½ small white cabbage, cored and shredded
2 tablespoons chopped pickled gherkins
8 black olives, stoned and chopped
DRESSING:
5 tablespoons olive or other salad oil
3–4 tablespoons lemon juice
1 teaspoon Dijon mustard
salt
freshly ground black pepper

Preparation time: 1 hour

1. Put the potatoes, celery, carrots, onion, cabbage, gherkins and olives in a salad bowl.
2. Put all the dressing ingredients in a screwtop jar and shake well. Adjust the seasoning, pour over the vegetables and toss well.

Serves 6 as a side salad

Nutrition content per serving   Carbohydrate: 25g   Fat: 13g
Fibre: 5g   Kilocalories: 221

CARROT & APPLE SALAD

350g (12oz) carrots, peeled and coarsely grated
3 Cox's Orange Pippin apples, cored and sliced
1 tablespoon lemon juice
1 tablespoon sunflower seeds
3 tablespoons raisins
2 teaspoons vegetable oil
2 tablespoons cashew nuts
FRENCH DRESSING:
4 tablespoons vegetable oil
2½ tablespoons cider vinegar or lemon juice
pinch of caster sugar
salt
freshly ground black pepper

Preparation time: 20 minutes

1. Put the grated carrot into a large bowl. Sprinkle the apple slices with lemon juice to prevent them discolouring, then add to the bowl with the sunflower seeds and raisins.

FROM TOP TO BOTTOM: Winter Vegetable Salad; Carrot & Apple Salad; Fennel, Apple & Raisin Salad; Sweet & Sour Cucumber.

2. Heat the oil in a small pan and lightly brown the cashew nuts. Lift out and drain on paper towels, then add to the bowl.
3. Put all the dressing ingredients in a screwtop jar and shake well to mix. Spoon over the salad and toss lightly. Serve immediately.

Serves 4 as a side salad

Nutrition content per serving   Carbohydrate: 25g   Fat: 28g
Fibre: 5g   Kilocalories: 351

FENNEL, APPLE & RAISIN SALAD

2 fennel bulbs, trimmed and thinly sliced
2 red dessert apples, cored and thinly sliced
2 tablespoons seedless raisins, to garnish
DRESSING:
150ml (¼ pint) soured cream
1 teaspoon cider vinegar
grated rind and juice of ½ orange
pinch of sugar
salt
freshly ground black pepper

Preparation time: 15 minutes

1. Mix together the dressing ingredients.
2. Toss together the fennel and apples in the dressing. Garnish the salad with the raisins.

Serves 4 as a side salad

Nutrition content per serving   Carbohydrate: 16g   Fat: 8g
Fibre: 4g   Kilocalories: 141

SWEET & SOUR CUCUMBER

1 firm, dark green cucumber
1 teaspoon salt
2 tablespoons caster sugar
2 tablespoons vinegar

Preparation time: 25–30 minutes

1. Split the cucumber in half lengthways, then cut it into strips rather like potato chips. Sprinkle with the salt and leave to drain for about 10 minutes, to extract the bitter juices.
2. Pat dry with paper towels and give each 'chip' a gentle pat with the side of a knife.
3. Place them on a serving dish. Sprinkle the sugar evenly over them and then the vinegar.

Serves 4 as a side salad

Nutrition content per serving   Carbohydrate: 10g   Fat: 0g
Fibre: 0g   Kilocalories: 41

PIQUANT POTATO SALAD

750g (1½lb) tiny new potatoes
salt
DRESSING:
3 tablespoons olive oil
1 tablespoon white wine vinegar
freshly ground black pepper
½ teaspoon made English mustard
2 teaspoons capers, finely chopped
1 pickled gherkin, finely chopped
1 tablespoon chopped fresh parsley

Preparation time: 5 minutes, plus cooling
Cooking time: 15–20 minutes

1. Wash the potatoes and place in a pan of boiling salted water. Cook for 15–20 minutes until just tender.
2. While the potatoes are cooking prepare the dressing. Put the oil and vinegar into a small bowl and stir in the salt, pepper, mustard, capers and gherkin. Add the chopped parsley.
3. Drain the potatoes well and tip them into a bowl. Pour the dressing over the hot potatoes and stir gently to coat them all thoroughly. Leave to cool, but do not chill.
4. Serve in a shallow dish at room temperature.

Serves 4 as a side salad

Nutrition content per serving   Carbohydrate: 35g   Fat: 12g
Fibre: 4g   Kilocalories: 247

WILTED SPINACH SALAD

450g (1lb) young fresh spinach, leaves only,
*   washed and dried*
50ml (2fl oz) olive oil
1 garlic clove, peeled and crushed
50g (2oz) canned water chestnuts, drained and
*   thinly sliced*
1 tablespoon soy sauce
2 tablespoons lemon juice or white wine vinegar
3 hard-boiled eggs, coarsely chopped

Preparation time: 5 minutes, plus chilling
Cooking time: about 8 minutes

1. Wrap the spinach leaves in a tea towel and put in the refrigerator to crisp.
2. Slowly heat the olive oil and garlic in a large saucepan for about 2 minutes (the garlic must not brown). Stir in the water chestnuts and soy sauce and cook for 1 minute longer.

3. Add the lemon juice and spinach. Turn the spinach over quickly until it is just wilted but not limp.
4. Place the spinach mixture in a glass bowl and scatter the chopped eggs on top. Serve at once.

Serves 4 as a side salad

Nutrition content per serving   Carbohydrate: 6g   Fat: 17g
Fibre: 3g   Kilocalories: 206

CELERIAC & CARROT REMOULADE

1 celeriac root, about 225g (8oz), peeled and
*   sliced into matchstick strips*
2 tablespoons lemon juice
225g (8oz) carrots, peeled and sliced into
*   matchstick strips*
salt
DRESSING:
4 tablespoons mayonnaise
150ml (¼ pint) plain Greek yogurt
1 garlic clove, peeled and crushed
1 tablespoon chopped fresh parsley
1 tablespoon finely snipped fresh chives
½ teaspoon mustard powder
pinch of cayenne pepper
1 hard-boiled egg, finely chopped
TO GARNISH:
1 hard-boiled egg, chopped
snipped fresh chives
carrot curls

Preparation time: 20 minutes, plus cooling
Cooking time: 10 minutes

1. Drop the celeriac strips as you cut them into a bowl of water acidulated with 1 tablespoon of lemon juice, to preserve their creamy colour.
2. Partly cook the celeriac and carrot strips for 5–8 minutes in boiling salted water with the remaining lemon juice. Drain, dry and cool the vegetables. (Reserve the flavoured stock for soup or a casserole.)
3. Mix the dressing ingredients. Taste and adjust the seasoning if necessary.
4. Toss the celeriac and carrots in the dressing and spoon the salad on to a serving dish. Garnish and serve.

Serves 4 as a side salad

Nutrition content per serving   Carbohydrate: 7g   Fat: 17g
Fibre: 4g   Kilocalories: 206

TOP: Piquant Potato Salad; MIDDLE: Wilted Spinach Salad; BOTTOM: Celeriac & Carrot Rémoulade.

CHINESE LEAF & BEAN SPROUT SALAD

2 tablespoons corn oil
1 tablespoon clear honey
1 tablespoon soy sauce
2 tablespoons lemon juice
100g (4oz) mushrooms, sliced
6 spring onions, chopped
100g (4oz) fresh bean sprouts
225g (8oz) Chinese leaves, coarsely shredded

Preparation time: 10 minutes

1. Pour the oil, honey, soy sauce and lemon juice to taste into a large bowl and mix well until well blended.
2. Add the sliced mushrooms to the soy dressing and mix until well coated and browned.
3. Stir in the spring onions and bean sprouts. Add the Chinese leaves and toss well.

Serves 4 as a side salad

Nutrition content per serving   Carbohydrate: 7g   Fat: 8g
Fibre: 3g   Kilocalories: 109

GREEN SALAD WITH ROQUEFORT DRESSING

Another French blue cheese with a creamy texture, such as Bresse Bleu or blue Brie, can be substituted for the Roquefort.

50g (2oz) Roquefort cheese
6 tablespoons olive oil
2 tablespoons garlic vinegar
2 tablespoons double cream (optional)
freshly ground black pepper
½ Webb's or iceberg lettuce, shredded
¼ curly endive, separated into sprigs

Preparation time: about 20 minutes

1. To make the dressing, crumble the cheese into a bowl, then mash with a fork, adding the oil a drop at a time to make a paste. Whisk in the vinegar and cream (if using), then add black pepper to taste. Set the dressing aside in a cool place.
2. Put the lettuce and endive in a large wide salad bowl and toss until evenly mixed.
3. Whisk the dressing vigorously, taste and adjust the seasoning, then pour over the salad.

Toss with salad servers until the salad is evenly coated with the dressing. Serve immediately.

Serves 4 as a side salad

Nutrition content per serving   Carbohydrate: 1g   Fat: 30g
Fibre: 1g   Kilocalories: 289

MUSHROOM & GRUYERE SALAD

225g (8oz) Gruyère cheese, cut into small cubes
100g (4oz) button mushrooms, quartered
4 large lettuce leaves
1 tablespoon finely chopped fresh parsley
DRESSING:
6 tablespoons olive oil
2 tablespoons red wine vinegar
1 garlic clove, peeled and crushed
½ teaspoon salt
large pinch of freshly ground black pepper

Preparation time: 30 minutes, plus marinating

1. Put all the dressing ingredients in a screw-topped jar and shake until well mixed.
2. Place the cheese and mushrooms in a mixing bowl and pour over the dressing. Toss to coat and leave for 20 minutes.
3. Line a shallow salad bowl with the lettuce leaves. Spoon the cheese mixture on top of the lettuce and sprinkle with the chopped parsley. Serve at once.

Serves 4 as a side salad

Nutrition content per serving   Carbohydrate: 0g   Fat: 42g
Fibre: 1g   Kilocalories: 438

TOP: Chinese Leaf & Bean Sprout Salad;
MIDDLE: Green Salad with Roquefort Dressing;
BOTTOM: Mushroom & Gruyère Salad.

SALAD NIÇOISE

1 firm round lettuce
3 firm tomatoes (skinned if preferred), quartered
2 hard-boiled eggs, quartered
6 anchovy fillets, halved lengthways
12 black olives
2 teaspoons capers
1 × 200g (7oz) can tuna fish in oil, drained
1 medium red pepper, cored, seeded and cut into
  strips
6 tablespoons good quality olive oil
1 large garlic clove, peeled and crushed
1 tablespoon chopped fresh tarragon
salt
freshly ground black pepper

Preparation time: 15–20 minutes

1. Keeping the lettuce whole, wash it well and shake dry. Remove the outer leaves and arrange them around the edge of a salad bowl; cut the remaining lettuce heart into quarters and place in the middle of the bowl.
2. Add the tomatoes, eggs, anchovies, olives, capers, tuna fish in chunks, and pepper strips.
3. Mix the oil with the garlic, tarragon, and salt and pepper to taste. Spoon the dressing evenly over the salad, and toss lightly before serving.

Serves 4 as a main dish

Nutrition content per serving   Carbohydrate: 3g   Fat: 37g
Fibre: 2g   Kilocalories: 412

POTATO, BEEF & TOMATO SALAD

1 small lettuce, separated into leaves
1 kg (2lb) cold roast beef, cubed
4 medium potatoes, cooked, peeled and cubed
4 medium tomatoes, skinned, seeded and quartered
4 pickled gherkins, sliced
SAUCE:
350ml (12fl oz) soured cream
3 tablespoons horseradish sauce
½ teaspoon salt
½ teaspoon white pepper

Preparation time: 45 minutes

1. Arrange the lettuce leaves on a large, shallow serving plate. Set aside.

TOP: Salad Niçoise; MIDDLE: Potato, Beef & Tomato Salad; BOTTOM: Chick Pea & Red Pepper Salad.

2. Mix the meat, potatoes, tomatoes and gherkins in a mixing bowl. Pile on the lettuce leaves.
3. Mix together the ingredients for the sauce and spoon over the meat mixture.

Serves 6 as a main dish

Nutrition content per serving   Carbohydrate: 18g   Fat: 28g
Fibre: 2g   Kilocalories: 535

CHICK PEA & RED PEPPER SALAD

175g (6oz) dried chick peas, soaked overnight
  and drained
2 red peppers
12 black olives
2 tablespoons chopped fresh coriander or parsley
parsley sprigs, to garnish
DRESSING:
3 tablespoons vegetable oil
½ teaspoon grated orange rind
2 tablespoons orange juice
1 garlic clove, peeled and crushed
salt
freshly ground black pepper

Preparation time: 15 minutes, plus soaking overnight and cooling
Cooking time: about 2 hours

1. Cook the chick peas in boiling unsalted water for 2 hours, or until they are tender. The actual length of the cooking time will depend on the 'age' of the pulses – how long they have been on the shelf.
2. Meanwhile, place the red peppers on a grill rack and cook them under a preheated moderate grill for about 20 minutes, turning them frequently until the skins are black and blistered. Hold the peppers under cold water then, using a small, sharp knife, peel off the skins. Halve the peppers, remove the core and seeds and thinly slice them.
3. Mix the dressing ingredients.
4. Drain the chick peas and toss in the dressing while they are still hot. Set aside to cool.
5. Stir in the peppers and olives and half the coriander. Turn the salad into a serving dish and sprinkle on the remaining coriander. Garnish with the sprigs of parsley.

Serves 4 as a side salad

Nutrition content per serving   Carbohydrate: 24g   Fat: 14g
Fibre: 7g   Kilocalories: 258

BREAD & CHEESE SALAD

4 thick slices day-old bread (brown or white)
150ml ($\frac{1}{4}$ pint) garlic dressing (see page 94)
1 teaspoon fresh thyme leaves
8 celery sticks, sliced crossways
4 tomatoes, cut into wedges
225g (8oz) hard cheese, e.g. Lancashire, Double
    Gloucester, Cheddar or Edam, cubed
lettuce or endive (optional)
celery leaves, to garnish

Preparation time: 15 minutes

1. Cut the bread into cubes, about 2cm ($\frac{3}{4}$ inch)
square, and place in a large bowl.
2. Mix the garlic dressing with the thyme and
pour over the bread. Toss to coat evenly.
3. Add the celery and tomatoes and toss lightly.
Add the cheese.
4. Serve straight from the bowl, or on a bed of
lettuce or endive, garnished with celery leaves.

Serves 4 as a main dish
Nutrition content per serving   Carbohydrate: 17g   Fat: 47g
Fibre: 5g   Kilocalories: 556

SPICY MEXICAN SALAD

1 × 312g (11oz) can sweetcorn kernels, drained
1 × 425g (15oz) can red kidney beans, drained
1 small onion, peeled and thinly sliced into rings
1 small green pepper, cored, seeded and sliced
175g (6oz) chorizo sausage, skinned and sliced
DRESSING:
4 tablespoons mayonnaise
2 tablespoons chilli relish
$\frac{1}{2}$ teaspoon mild chilli powder
1 tablespoon finely chopped red pepper
pinch of salt

Preparation time: 20 minutes, plus chilling

1. In a large salad bowl, mix the sweetcorn,
kidney beans, onion rings, green pepper and
chorizo sausage, tossing gently to mix.
2. Mix the mayonnaise with the chilli relish,
chilli powder, red pepper and salt.
3. Just before serving, spoon the dressing over
the salad ingredients and toss well to mix.
Serve with tortillas or corn chips.

Serves 4 as a main dish
Nutrition content per serving   Carbohydrate: 60g   Fat: 34g
Fibre: 28g   Kilocalories: 655

BROAD BEAN SALAD WITH SALAMI

1.5kg (3$\frac{1}{2}$lb) fresh young broad beans, shelled
150g (5oz) French or Italian salami, cut into
    slices 3mm ($\frac{1}{8}$ inch) thick, rinds removed,
    chopped
8 tablespoons olive oil
2 tablespoons lemon juice
freshly ground black pepper
150g (5oz) feta cheese, crumbled

Preparation time: 30 minutes

1. Put the beans and salami into a large bowl.
Pour in the olive oil and lemon juice and mix
thoroughly, then season with pepper.
2. Sprinkle the feta cheese on top. No salt is
needed as the feta is already salty.

Serves 6 as a main dish
Nutrition content per serving   Carbohydrate: 6g   Fat: 37g
Fibre: 4g   Kilocalories: 405

SMOKED TROUT & ORANGE SALAD

350g (12oz) smoked trout fillets, skinned and
    boned
$\frac{1}{2}$ cucumber, very thinly sliced
3 oranges, peeled, pith removed and segmented
3 celery sticks, thinly sliced
salad leaves, to garnish
DRESSING:
40g (1$\frac{1}{2}$oz) dessert apple, grated
1 tablespoon lemon juice
3 tablespoons mayonnaise
1$\frac{1}{2}$ teaspoons creamed horseradish

Preparation time: 20 minutes, plus chilling

1. Mix the dressing ingredients together.
2. Flake the smoked trout into bite-sized pieces.
Place in a mixing bowl with the cucumber,
orange segments and celery and toss to mix.
3. To serve, line a serving dish with salad
leaves. Top with the smoked trout salad and
spoon over the dressing.

Serves 4 as a main dish
Nutrition content per serving   Carbohydrate: 11g   Fat: 14g
Fibre: 3g   Kilocalories: 241

FROM TOP TO BOTTOM: Bread & Cheese Salad;
Spicy Mexican Salad; Broad Bean Salad with Salami;
Smoked Trout & Orange Salad.

TUSCAN SALAD

225g (8oz) long-grain rice
4 tablespoons dry white wine
1 green pepper, cored, seeded and thinly sliced
1 red pepper, cored, seeded and thinly sliced
1 × 100g (4oz) can fagioli or other beans,
  drained
1 small cucumber, peeled and diced
10 stuffed green olives, halved
2 spring onions, thinly sliced
fresh basil sprigs, to garnish
DRESSING:
6 tablespoons olive oil
3 tablespoons red wine vinegar
1 teaspoon dried basil
1 garlic clove, peeled and crushed
1 teaspoon salt
½ teaspoon freshly ground black pepper

Preparation time: 30 minutes, plus cooling and chilling
Cooking time: 15 minutes

1. Cook the rice in boiling salted water for 15 minutes or until tender. Drain well. Put in a mixing bowl and stir in the wine. Cool.
2. Put the green and red peppers, beans, cucumber, olives and spring onions in a salad bowl. When the rice is cold, add it to the vegetable mixture and stir well.
3. Mix together the dressing ingredients in a screw-topped jar. Add to the rice mixture and toss to coat thoroughly. Chill for 30 minutes, tossing occasionally. Serve garnished with basil.

Serves 4 as a main dish

Nutrition content per serving   Carbohydrate: 55g   Fat: 24g
Fibre: 4g   Kilocalories: 453

SARDINE SALAD

2 dessert apples
juice of ½ lemon
75g (3oz) Edam or Gouda cheese, diced
handful of broken walnuts, finely chopped
150ml (¼ pint) soured cream
salt
freshly ground black pepper
2 × 100g (4oz) cans sardines in oil, drained
salad greens, to finish
parsley sprig, to garnish

Preparation time: 40 minutes

1. Peel and core the apples, then chop finely. Put in a bowl and sprinkle with the lemon juice, then add the cheese, walnuts, soured cream and salt and pepper to taste. Stir well to mix. Gently fold in the sardines.
2. Spoon on to a large plate or dish, on or next to salad greens. Garnish with parsley.

Variation: Any canned fish in oil can be used instead of the sardines – try mackerel, brisling or pilchards.

Serves 4 as a main dish

Nutrition content per serving   Carbohydrate: 10g   Fat: 40g
Fibre: 1g   Kilocalories: 457

SPINACH NOODLE & HAM SALAD

225g (8oz) green spinach noodles
salt
100g (4oz) mushrooms, thinly sliced
225g (8oz) cooked ham, thinly sliced
25g (1oz) Parmesan cheese, grated
fresh oregano sprig, to garnish
GARLIC DRESSING:
6 tablespoons olive oil
3½ tablespoons lemon juice
1 small garlic clove, peeled and crushed
salt
freshly ground black pepper

Preparation time: 5 minutes, plus cooling
Cooking time: 15 minutes

1. Add the noodles to a large pan of boiling salted water and cook for 10–15 minutes until tender but not soft (al dente). Drain.
2. Put the dressing ingredients in a large mixing bowl and whisk together well. Add the mushrooms. Toss until the mushrooms are well coated. Add the noodles while still warm and toss again.
3. Cut the ham into ribbons about the same width as the noodles, add to the salad and toss together.
4. To serve, transfer to a large bowl, sprinkle with Parmesan and garnish with a sprig of oregano.

Serves 4 as a main dish

Nutrition content per serving   Carbohydrate: 40g   Fat: 31g
Fibre: 4g   Kilocalories: 500

TOP: Tuscan Salad; MIDDLE: Sardine Salad;
BOTTOM: Spinach Noodle & Ham Salad.

INDEX